LEGAL ATTACK

Chess – An Intellectual Board War

K A R T H I K   M U R U G A N

Tactics, Traps and Tips

Archway Publishing books may be ordered through booksellers or by contacting:

Archway Publishing
1663 Liberty Drive
Bloomington, IN 47403
www.archwaypublishing.com
844-669-3957

ISBN: 978-1-4808-9721-2 (sc)
ISBN: 978-1-4808-9722-9 (e)

Library of Congress Control Number: 2020919245

Print information available on the last page.

Archway Publishing rev. date: 12/28/2020

CONTENTS

ACKNOWLEDGMENTS

I want to thank NM Matthew O'Brien for guiding me and reviewing the chess content of this book. Mr. O'Brien is a National Master and one of the top chess players in the state of Pennsylvania.

Many thanks to Mr. Mark M. Wood, president of Wood Chess Club, for introducing chess to me, and my coaches—Mr. Joshua Anderson, president of the Tri-Bridges Chess Club, and NM Mr. Peter Minear—for taking me further through my chess journey. Mr. Minear is a four-time Pennsylvania state champion.

Thanks to Mrs. Deborah Kearney for her help with editing this book. Mrs. Kearney is the vice principal at Lionville Elementary School, Downingtown, Pennsylvania.

I also want to thank my dad, Saravanan Murugan, for bringing a shape to this book and supporting me all the way. Without the support and encouragement of each of these people, my book would not be the same.

INTRODUCTION

This book is intended for players who are starting their journey in chess and are interested and preparing themselves to play with players around 1000 Chess Federation rating.

It starts by introducing chess basics and then shifts its focus to puzzles. This book has 300 chess puzzles categorized under 30 powerful chess tactics. Each tactic has 10 puzzles. The first two puzzles are examples with arrows indicating the solution. The next eight puzzles are for the reader to solve. Practicing these puzzles will help recognize standard patterns to improve and win your games. Puzzles are organized from simple to more complex, gradually taking the reader through the important aspects of chess. Puzzles focus on tactics, mates, and traps. The solutions to all the tactics and quizzes are at the end of the book. Refer to them anytime you see fit. Mastering these tactics could help you win many games.

Almost all games experienced players play is decided by a tactical blunder, usually the loss of a full piece.—Bruce Alberston.

In my opinion, tactics are the most important things to know in chess.—Karthik Murugan

CHAPTER 1
CHESS BASICS

CHESS IS A mind sport that involves constant thinking, planning, and strategy. It is a two-player game in which each player has sixteen pieces on a sixty-four-square board. Chess was invented in India in the sixth century AD, but it was the Persians who made the more modern version of chess that we play today.

The chessboard consists of ranks, files, and diagonals. The ranks are horizontal and the files are vertical. There are eight ranks and eight files, and their notation begins from white's side. The ranks are denoted by number, and the files go by letter. The ranks go from 1 to 8 and files a to h.

Pawns are placed on the second and seventh ranks. Rooks go in the corners. Knights go next to the rooks. The bishops are placed next to the knights. The queen always goes on its own color. Then the king sits next to it. White always starts play.

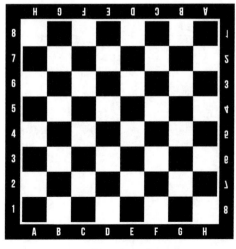

Chessboard

There are three possible results of a chess game: win, loss, or draw. There are four ways to win a game: checkmate, resignation, flag, or forfeit. Checkmate is when an opponent's king is under check, and the player cannot make any other legal move. Resignation is when a player is sure to lose and quits the game early by saying, "I resign." Flagging is when a player runs out of time on the clock. Forfeit results when one player either cheats or does not show up to the game. That player automatically loses.

There are three ways to get a draw: stalemate, draw offered and accepted, or three-move repetition. Stalemate results when one player has zero possible moves and is not in check. A draw can be offered by playing the move, then offering the draw and hitting the clock. The opponent has a choice of whether to accept or not. Three-move repetition results when a player repeats the same position three times.

Chess Pieces

	PAWN	1 point
	BISHOP	3 points
	KNIGHT	3 points
	ROOK	5 points
	QUEEN	9 points
	KING	The Game

The King

The king is the most valuable piece on the chessboard. It can move exactly one vacant square in any direction: forward, backward, left, right, or diagonal. The king also has a special move called *castling*, in which it moves two squares toward one of its own rooks and, in the same move, the rook jumps over the king to land on the square on the king's other side. The king is passive in the opening and middle game but becomes stronger in the endgame. The objective of chess is to checkmate the opponent's king.

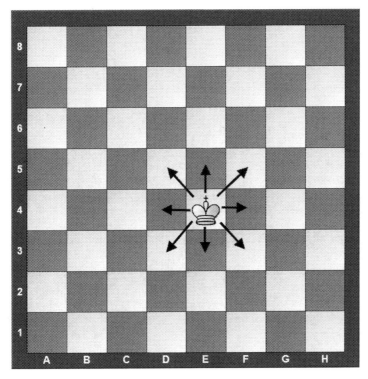

King Movement

The Queen

The queen is the most powerful piece. The white queen starts on a white square and the black queen starts on a black square. The queen stands next to the king at the start of the game. It can move any number of vacant squares in any direction—forward, backward, left, right, or diagonal—in a straight line. Losing the queen is least desirable situation next to checkmate.

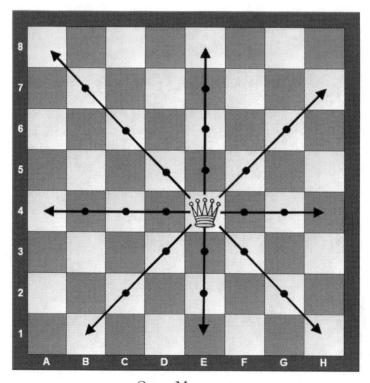

Queen Movement

The Rook

The rook is a major piece that moves in straight lines. The white rooks start on squares a1 and h1, while the black rooks start on a8 and h8. Rooks can move horizontally or vertically through any number of unoccupied squares (see diagram). As with other pieces, the rook captures by occupying the square on which the enemy piece sits. The rook also participates in castling.

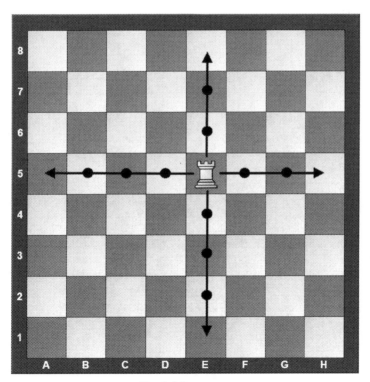

Rook Movement

The Bishop

The bishop is a minor piece that can move diagonally in any direction on its color. The bishop has no restrictions in distance for each move.

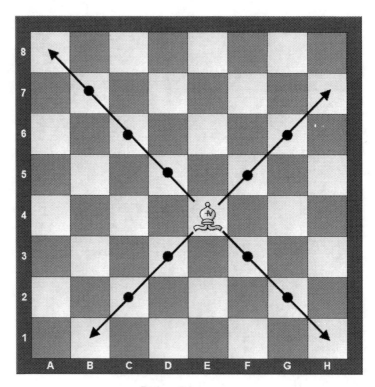

Bishop Movement

The Knight

The knight is a minor piece that moves in an L-shape. Knights move unlike any other chess piece. Rather than moving up and down or side to side, the knight jumps, which makes it a very dangerous and powerful piece in the chess game. Knights are the only chess pieces that can jump over other chess pieces.

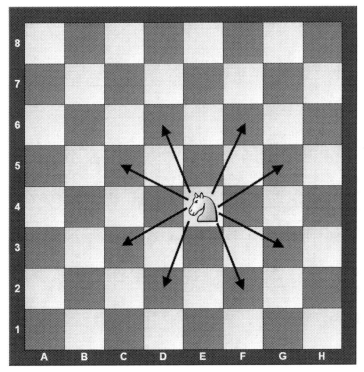

Knight Movement

The Pawn

The pawn is the most abundant piece on the chessboard. On its first move, a pawn can advance two squares. After a specific pawn's first movement, it can move only one square forward at a time. Pawns capture diagonally. They are often described as the weakest pieces on the chessboard, but they usually outlast all the other pieces in endgames. Once a pawn gets to the other end of the chessboard, it can be promoted to any piece but the king and the pawn itself.

Pawn Movement

STAGES OF CHESS

The Opening

The *opening* refers to the moves of the game until the minor pieces are developed and both rooks are connected. There are three objectives in the opening. The first is to control the center. The next is to develop your pieces. The last is to give the king safety. These objectives will guarantee a good position in the game.

The Middle Game

The *middle game* is when most of the action takes place. Most games are decided in this stage. Both players are constantly trying to gain the advantage. Most tactics are usually played in the middle game. The players put tremendous pressure on each other. Many attacks start in the opening but ripen in the middle game. Then, after gaining an advantage, players try to convert to a winning endgame.

The Endgame

The *endgame* is the portion of the game with few pieces left on the chessboard. Whoever is better at leaving the middle game usually wins the endgame. In endgames, players need to play like machines and not make any mistakes. The slightest miscalculated move order or mix-up could cost a player the game. Conversion in endgames is key to winning. Once a player is up material or has a better position, that player needs to convert the advantage into a win.

Chess Notation

Chess notation is very simple to learn. You record the first letter of the piece that is moving and then the letter and number square where it is placed. Players do not mention the pawn in notation; they just mention the letter and number square.

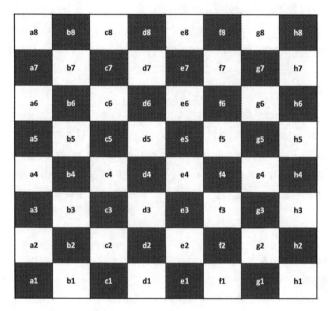

Chess Board - Square Names

Symbols

- K = King
- Q = Queen
- R = Rook
- B = Bishop
- N = Knight
- P = Pawn (Although, by convention, P is usually omitted while notating)
- x = Captures
- 0-0 = Kingside castle
- 0-0-0 = Queenside castle
- + = Check
- # = Checkmate
- Pe8 = Q (Pawn Promotion)

Chess Quiz 1

1. How many squares are there on the board?
2. How many pieces are there in total?
3. Which side moves first?
4. What letter shape does the knight move in?
5. In what direction does the pawn capture?
6. What happens when a pawn reaches the other end of the board?
7. What are three different ways to win a game?
8. What color does the white queen start on?
9. What two pieces can move on the first move?
10. How do you win when your opponent plays until the end?

CHAPTER 2
BASIC CHESS PUZZLES

♜ ♞ ♝ ♚ ♛ ♞ ♙

1. Fork

A *fork* is a tactic in which a single piece makes two or more direct attacks simultaneously. The fork is one of the most basic and most common tactics in the game of chess.

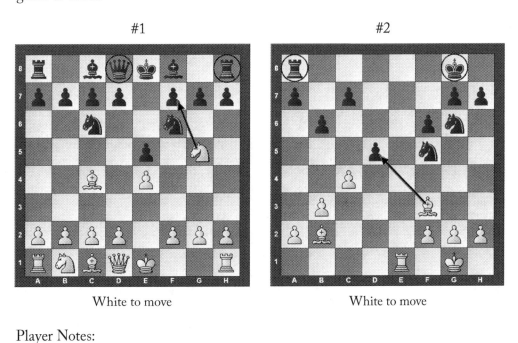

#1   #2

White to move   White to move

Player Notes:

- -

- -

- -

#3

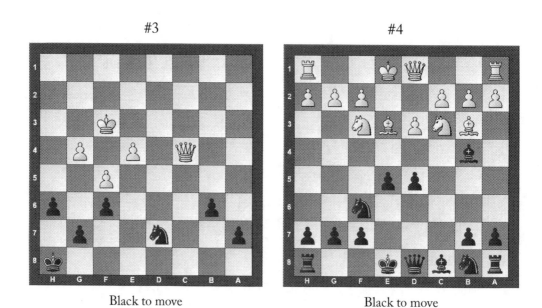

Black to move

#4

Black to move

#5

White to move

#6

Black to move

#7

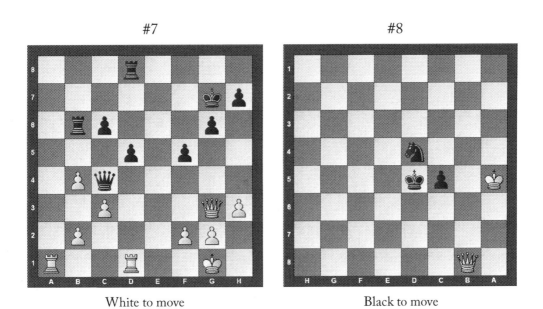

White to move

#8

Black to move

#9

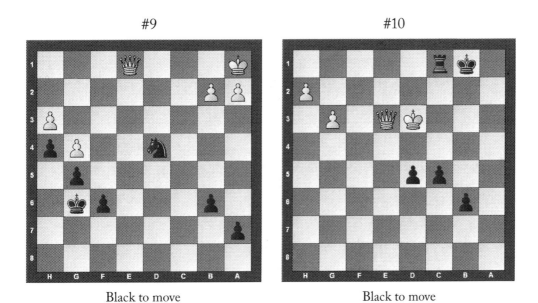

Black to move

#10

Black to move

2. Pin

A *pin* is a situation, brought on by an attacking piece, in which a defending piece cannot move without exposing a more valuable defending piece on its other side to capture by the attacking piece.

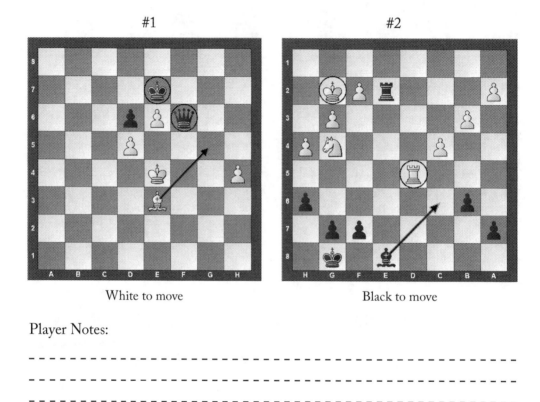

          #1   #2

White to move   Black to move

Player Notes:

#3

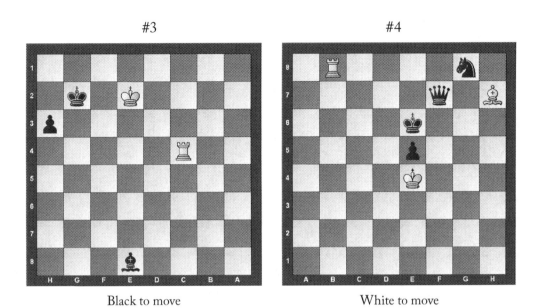

Black to move

#4

White to move

#5

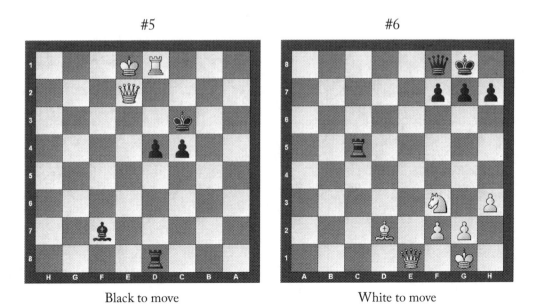

Black to move

#6

White to move

#7

#8

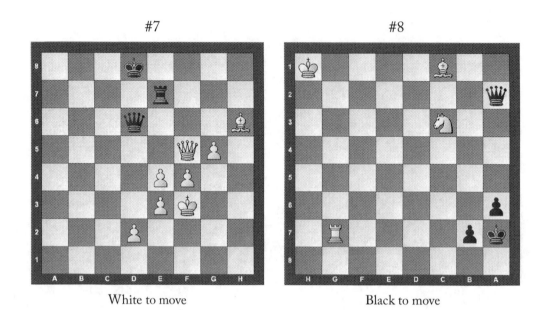

White to move

Black to move

#9

#10

Black to move

Black to move

3. Skewer

A *skewer* is an attack upon two pieces in a line and is similar to a pin. A skewer is sometimes described as a *reverse pin*. The difference is that in a skewer, the more valuable piece is the one under direct attack.

#1   #2

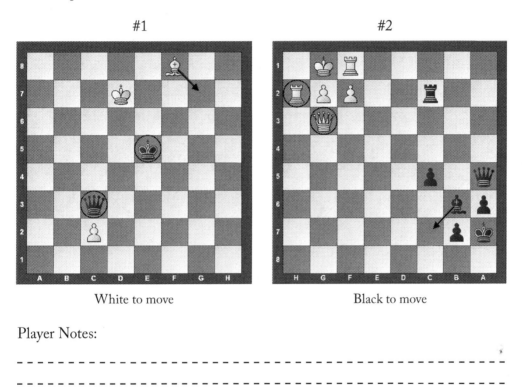

White to move   Black to move

Player Notes:

- -
- -
- -

#3

#4

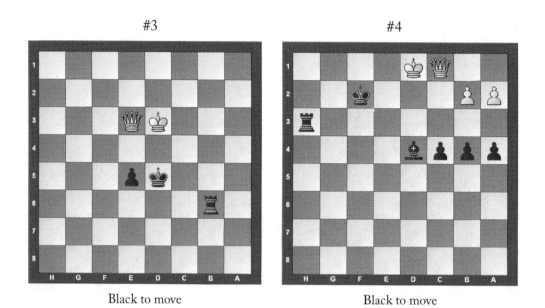

Black to move   Black to move

#5

#6

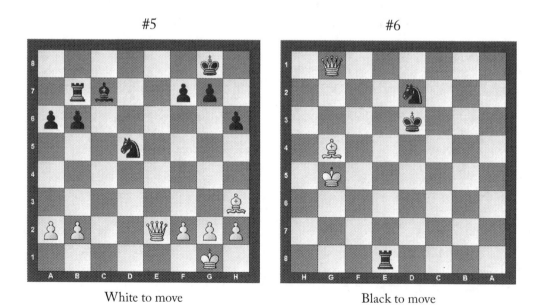

White to move   Black to move

#7

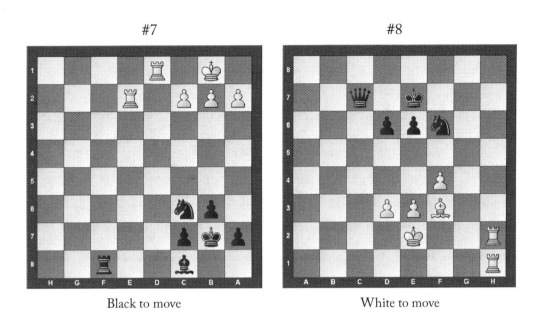

Black to move

#8

White to move

#9

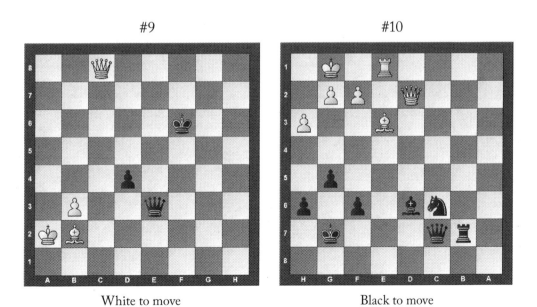

White to move

#10

Black to move

4. Discovered Attack

A *discovered attack* is an attack revealed when one piece moves out of the way of another. A discovered attack can be extremely powerful, as the piece moved can make a threat independent of the piece it reveals.

#1   #2

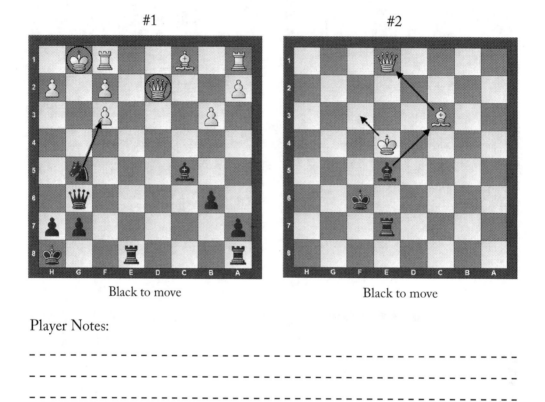

Black to move   Black to move

Player Notes:

#3

#4

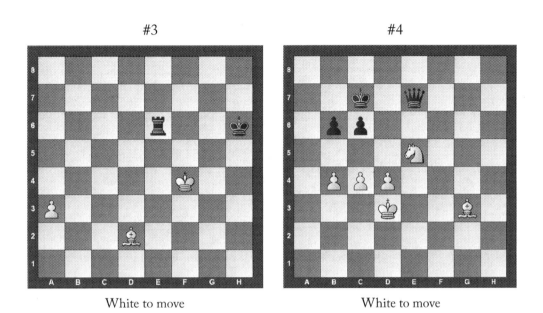

White to move

White to move

#5

#6

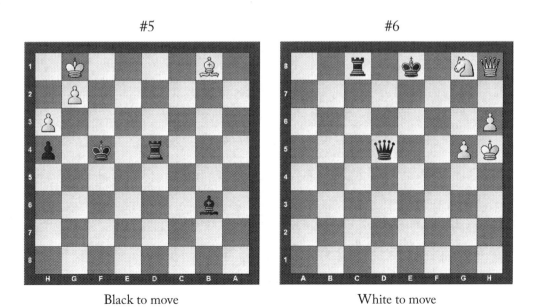

Black to move

White to move

#7

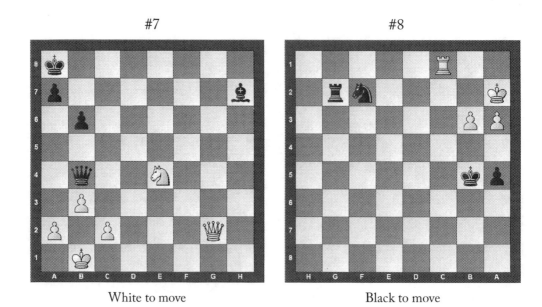

White to move

#8

Black to move

#9

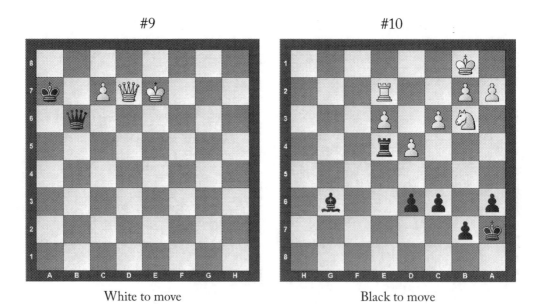

White to move

#10

Black to move

5. Back Rank

These are tactics and mates happening on first and eighth ranks of the chessboard.

#1

White to move

#2

Black to move

Player Notes:

- -

- -

- -

#3

#4

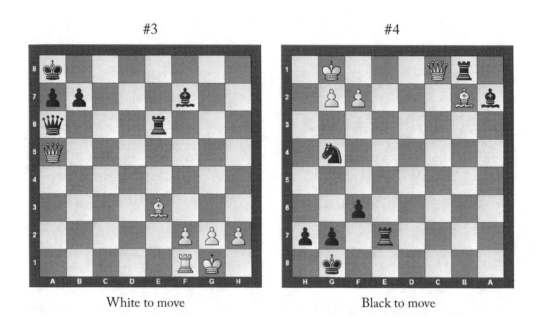

White to move   Black to move

#5

#6

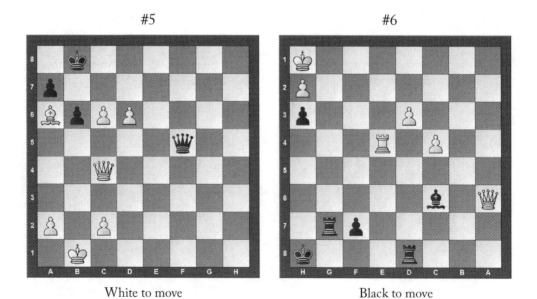

White to move   Black to move

#7

#8

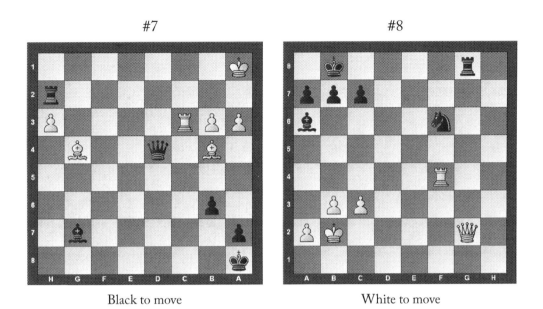

Black to move

White to move

#9

#10

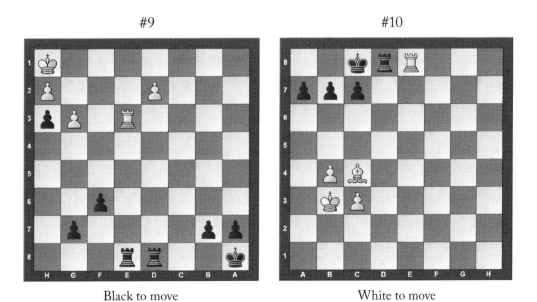

Black to move

White to move

6. Deflection

Deflection is when a player redirects the opponent's pieces to benefit the player's position.

#1   #2

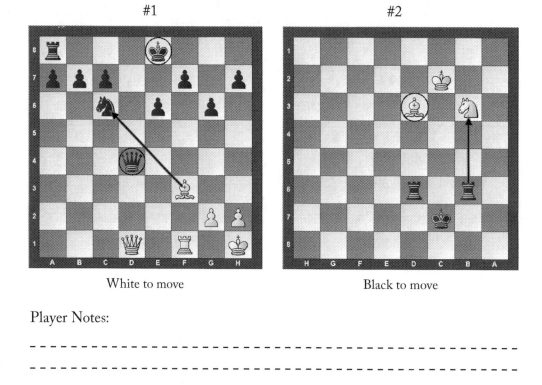

White to move   Black to move

Player Notes:

- -

- -

- -

#3

#4

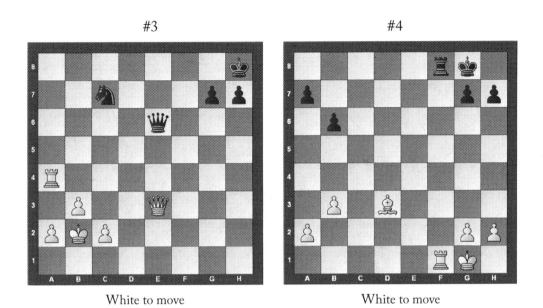

White to move   White to move

#5

#6

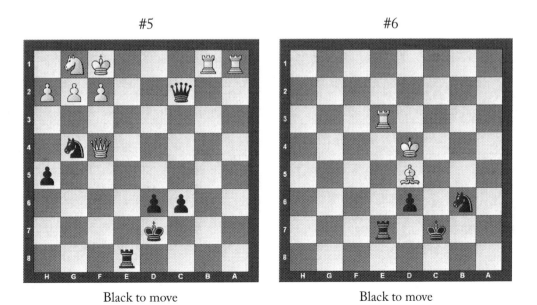

Black to move   Black to move

#7

#8

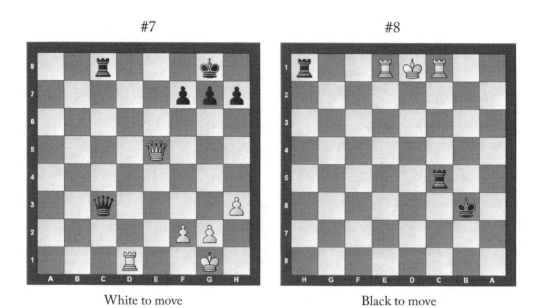

White to move   Black to move

#9

#10

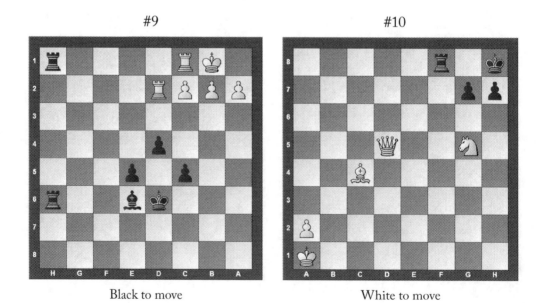

Black to move   White to move

7. Clearance

Clearance is when a player clears a file or rank, enabling the player's pieces to do more than they were originally doing.

#1

#2

Black to move

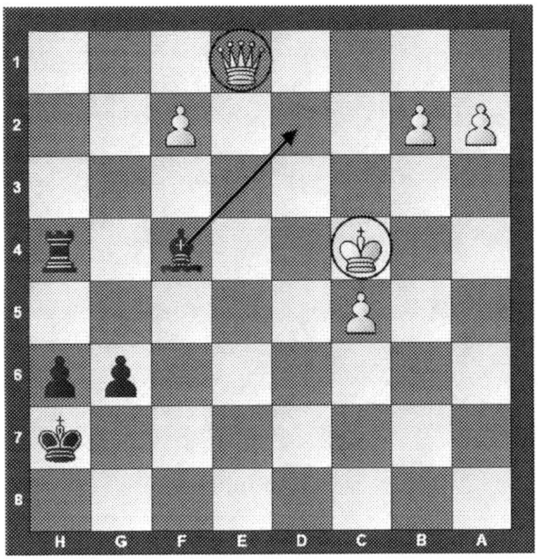

Black to move

Player Notes:

_____

_____

_____

#3

#4

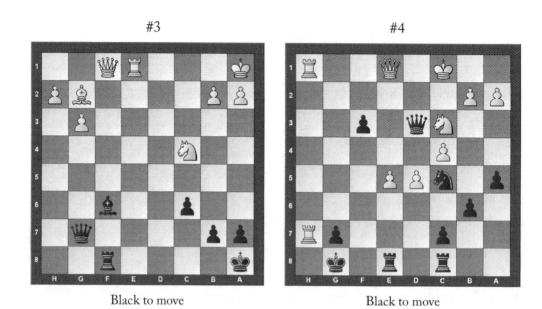

Black to move   Black to move

#5

#6

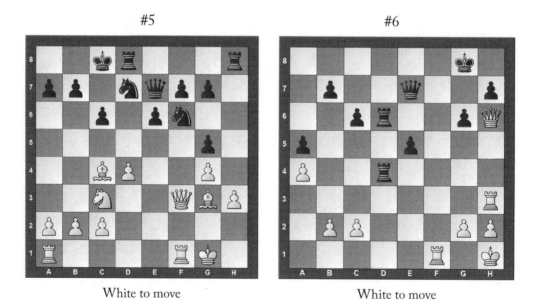

White to move   White to move

#7

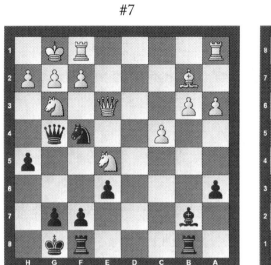

Black to move

#8

White to move

#9

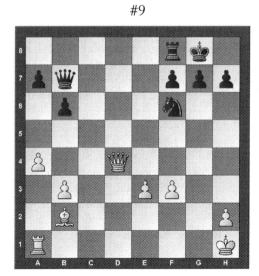

White to move

#10

Black to move

8. Pawn Promotion

These are tactics that involve a pawn being pushed to the eighth rank for white or first rank for black to upgrade that pawn to another piece.

#1   #2

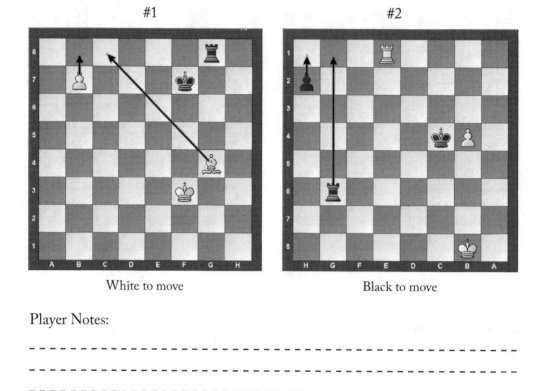

White to move   Black to move

Player Notes:

- -

- -

- -

#3

#4

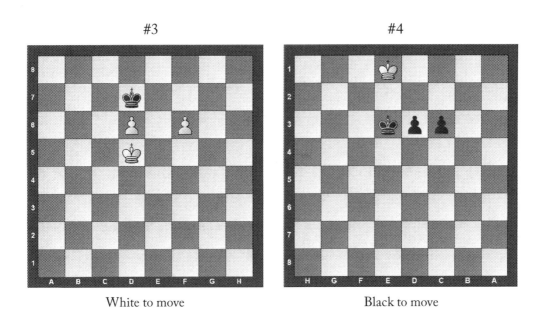

White to move   Black to move

#5

#6

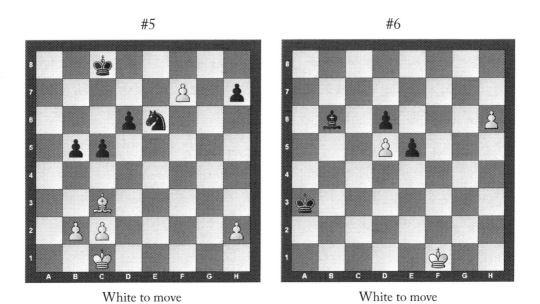

White to move   White to move

#7   #8

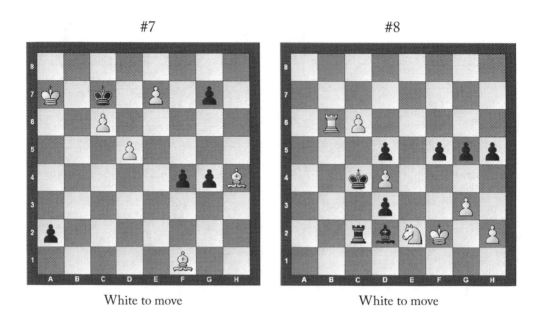

White to move   White to move

#9   #10

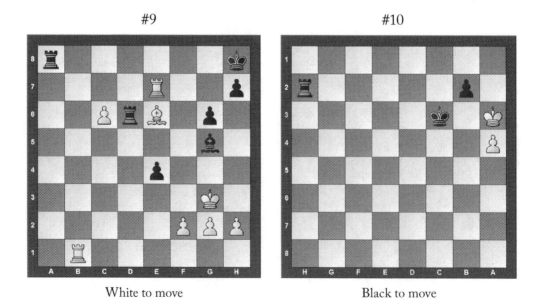

White to move   Black to move

9. Basic Pawn Endings

These are must-know pawn endings that could decide if the game result is a win, draw, or loss.

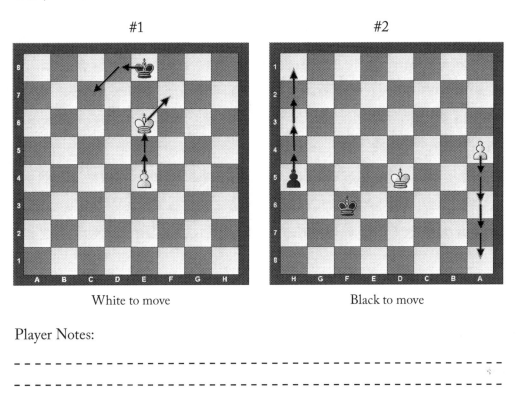

#1   #2

White to move   Black to move

Player Notes:

- -

- -

- -

#3

#4

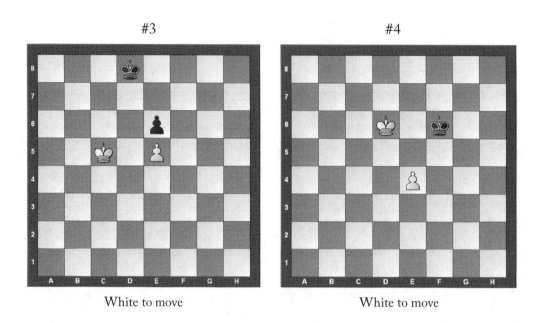

White to move

White to move

#5

#6

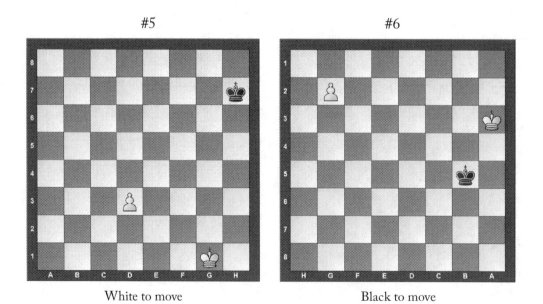

White to move

Black to move

#7

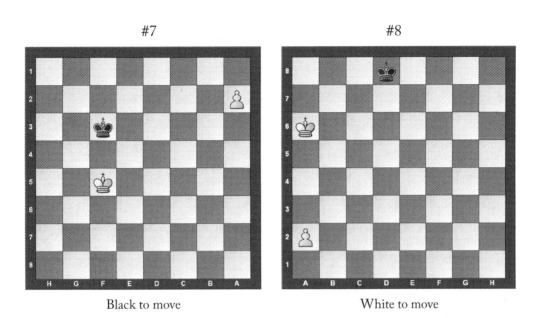

Black to move

#8

White to move

#9

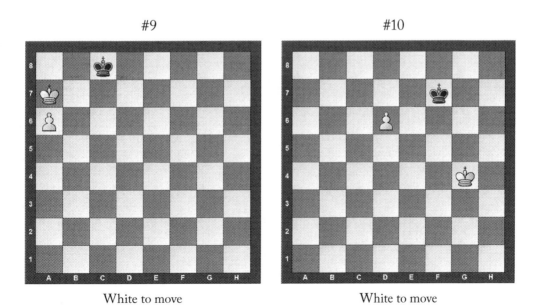

White to move

#10

White to move

10. Trapped Piece

This tactic occurs when the opponent's piece cannot escape from attack and therefore is lost.

#1   #2

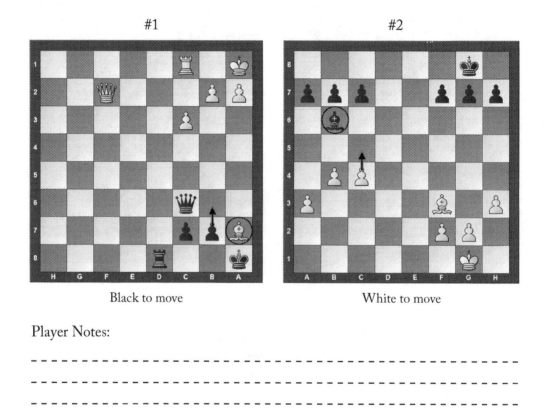

Black to move   White to move

Player Notes:

- -

- -

- -

#3

#4

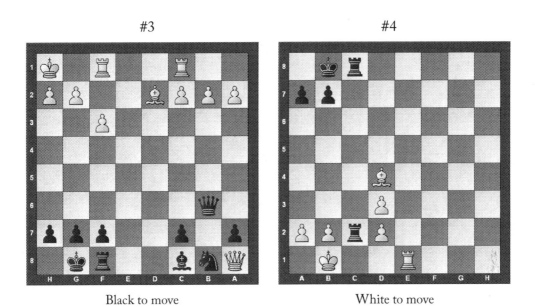

Black to move   White to move

#5

#6

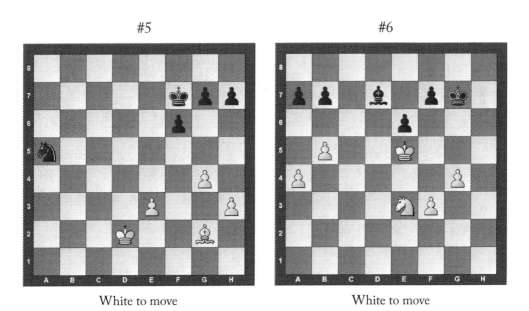

White to move   White to move

#7

#8

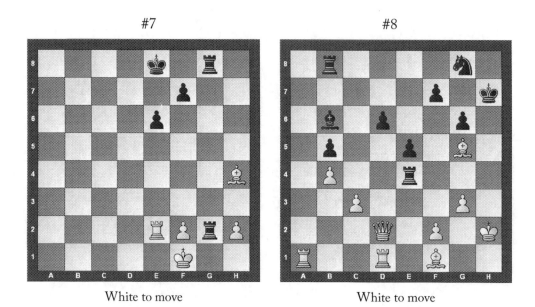

White to move

White to move

#9

#10

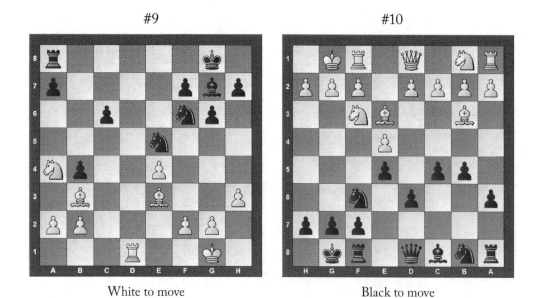

White to move

Black to move

Chess Quiz 2

1. What is a fork?
2. What is the only piece that jumps over other pieces?
3. What happens when the only remaining pieces on the board are the two kings?
4. What pieces can you promote your pawn to?
5. Which tactic uses redirection?
6. Which tactic reveals an attack once a piece moves?
7. Which tactic threatens two pieces at the same time?
8. What is the difference between a pin and a skewer?
9. What three pieces can deliver a pin?
10. What two pieces can deliver a diagonal skewer?

CHAPTER 3
CHECKMATES

11. Basic Mates

These are must-know checkmates that could come in very handy in certain situations.

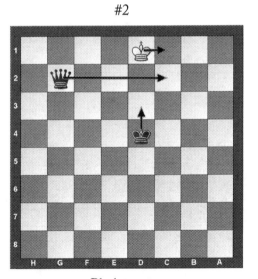

#1   #2

Black to move   Black to move

Player Notes:

#3

#4

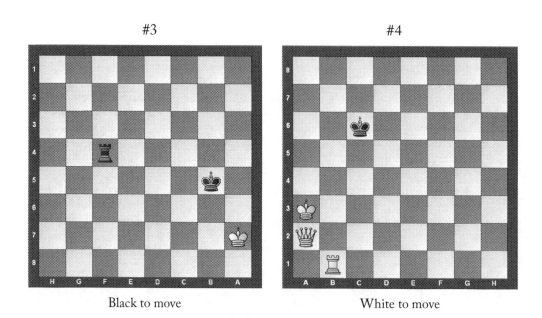

Black to move   White to move

#5

#6

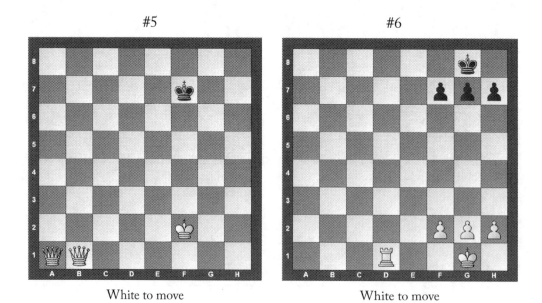

White to move   White to move

#7

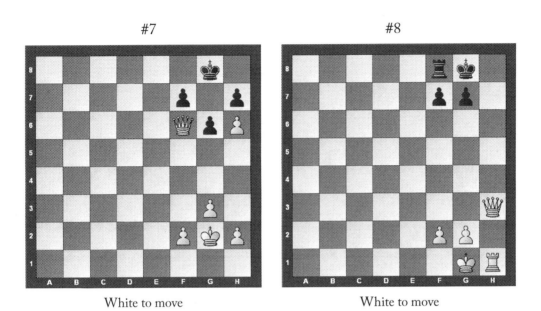

White to move

#8

White to move

#9

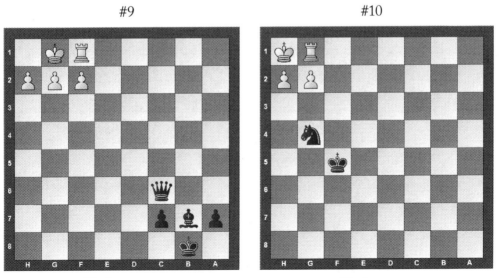

Black to move

#10

Black to move

12. Mate in One

A *mate in one* is a checkmate conducted in one move.

#1   #2

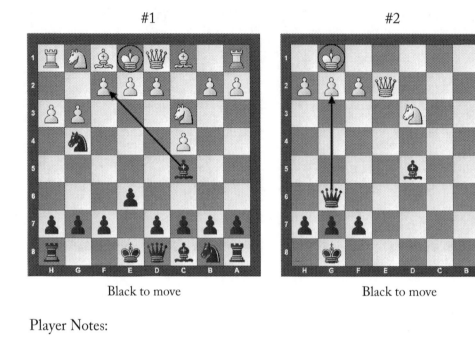

Black to move   Black to move

Player Notes:

- -

- -

- -

#3

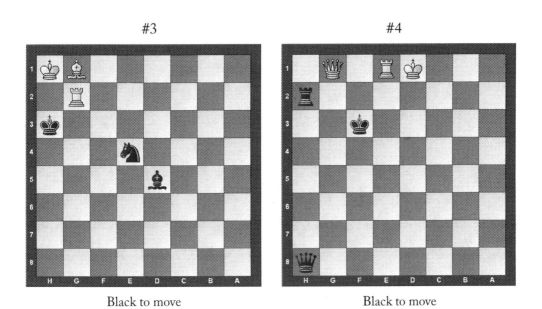

Black to move

#4

Black to move

#5

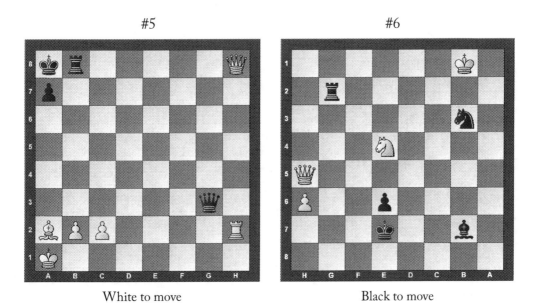

White to move

#6

Black to move

#7

#8

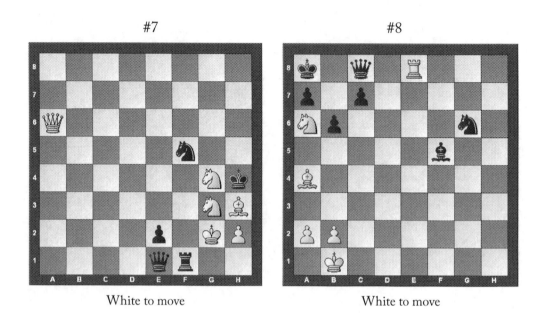

White to move   White to move

#9

#10

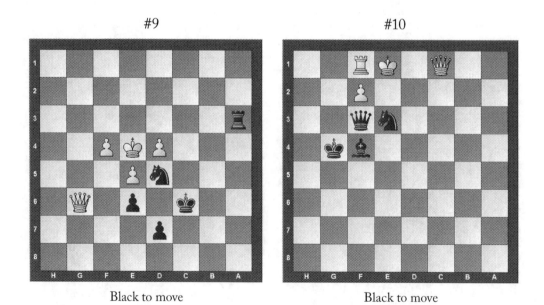

Black to move   Black to move

13. Mate in Two

A *mate in two* is a checkmate that is achieved in two moves.

#1

#2

White to move   White to move

Player Notes:

#3

#4

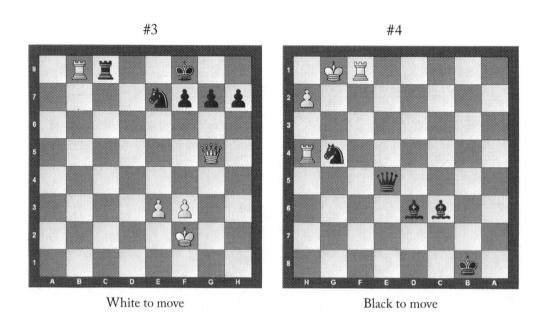

White to move

Black to move

#5

#6

Black to move

Black to move

#7

#8

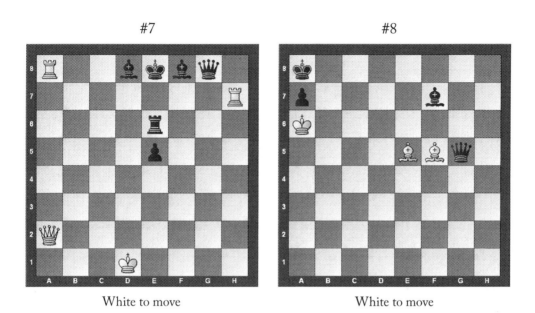

White to move   White to move

#9

#10

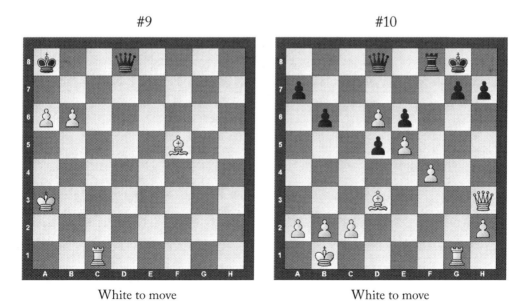

White to move   White to move

14. Queen Mate

A *queen mate* is a checkmate that is conducted by a queen.

#1   #2

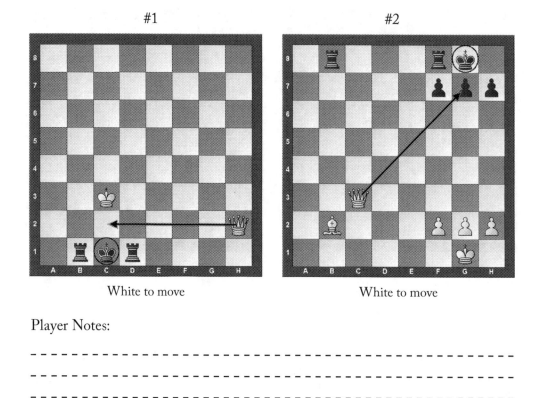

White to move   White to move

Player Notes:

- -

- -

- -

#3

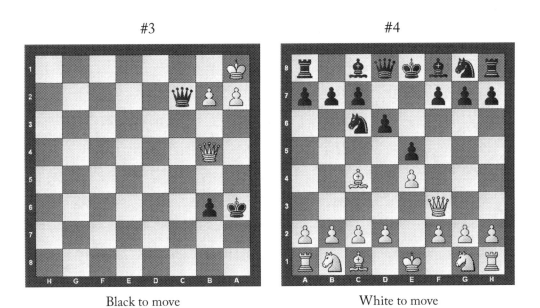

Black to move

#4

White to move

#5

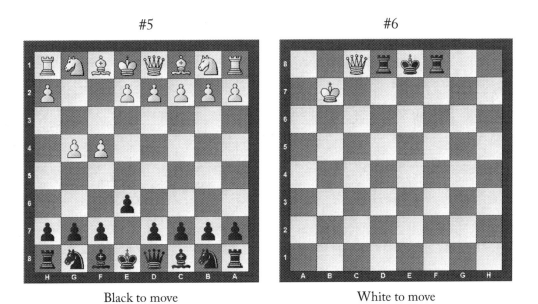

Black to move

#6

White to move

#7

#8

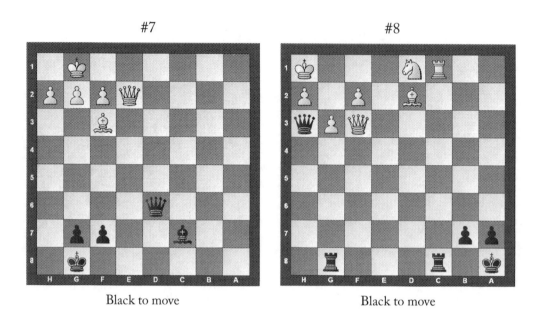

Black to move

Black to move

#9

#10

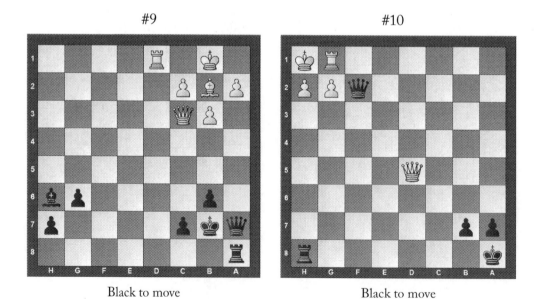

Black to move

Black to move

15. Rook Mate

A *rook mate* is a checkmate that is conducted by a rook.

#1

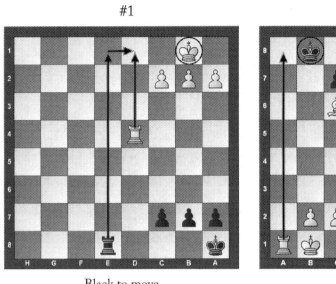

Black to move

#2

White to move

Player Notes:

- -

- -

- -

#3

#4

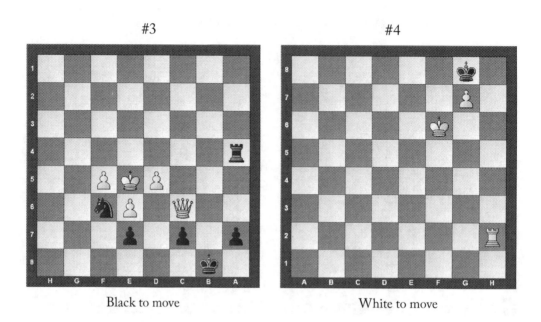

Black to move

White to move

#5

#6

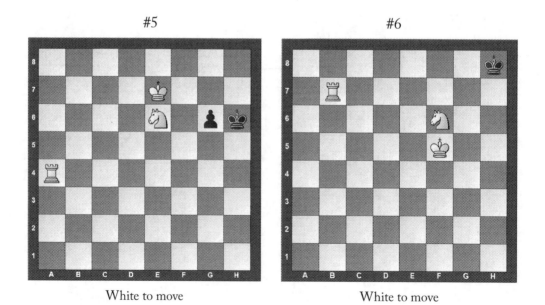

White to move

White to move

#7

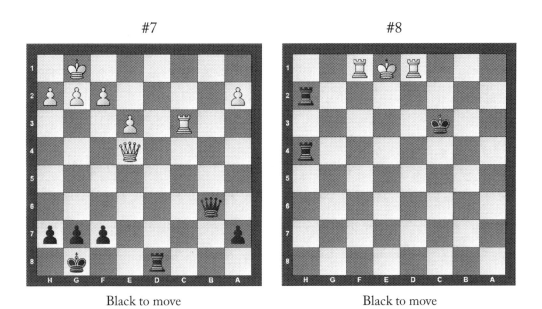

Black to move

#8

Black to move

#9

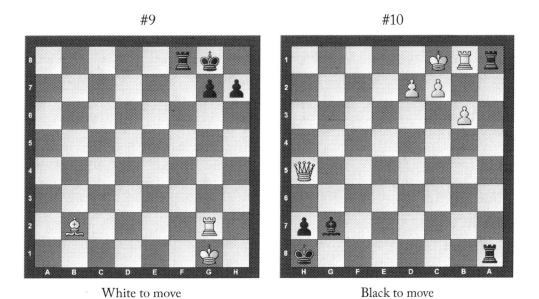

White to move

#10

Black to move

16. Bishop Mate

A *bishop mate* is a checkmate conducted by a bishop.

#1   #2

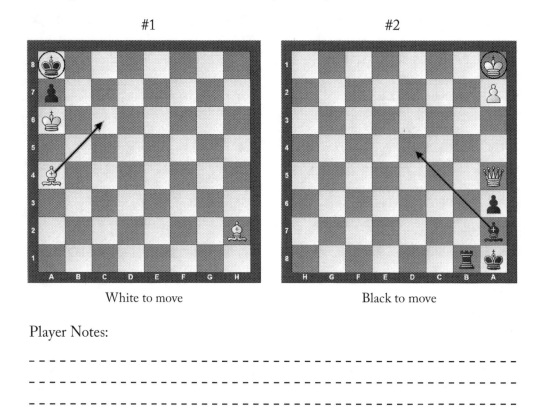

White to move   Black to move

Player Notes:

- -

- -

- -

#3

#4

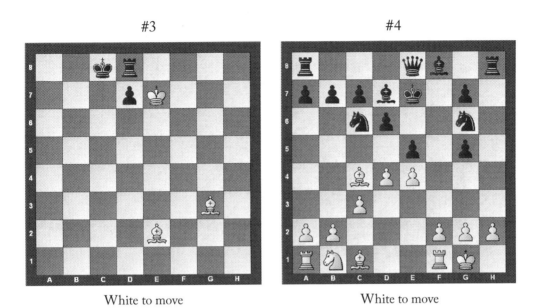

White to move

White to move

#5

#6

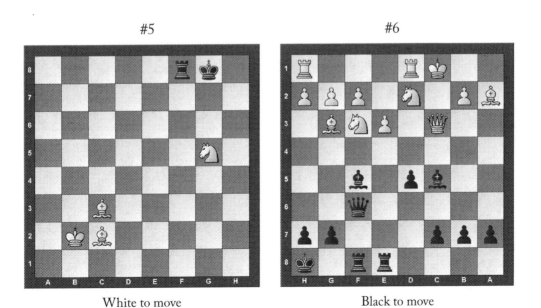

White to move

Black to move

#7

#8

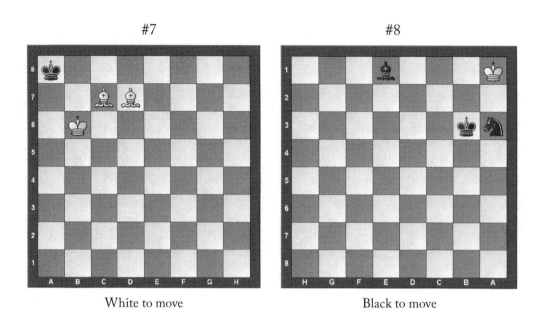

White to move

Black to move

#9

#10

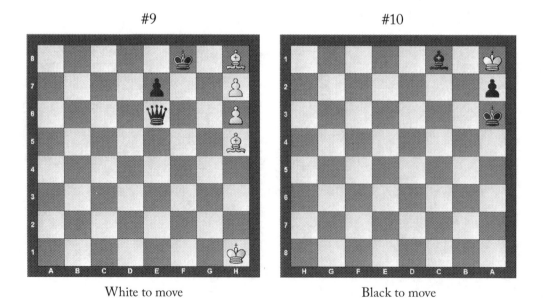

White to move

Black to move

17. Knight Mate

A *knight mate* is a checkmate that is delivered by a knight.

#1   #2

White to move   White to move

Player Notes:

- -

- -

- -

#3

#4

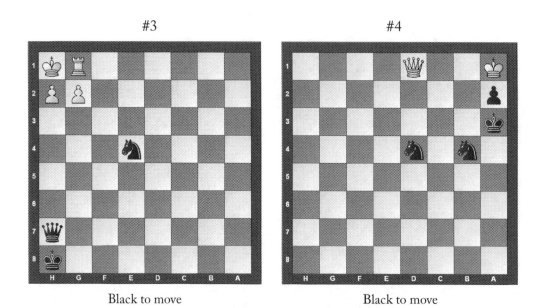

Black to move   Black to move

#5

#6

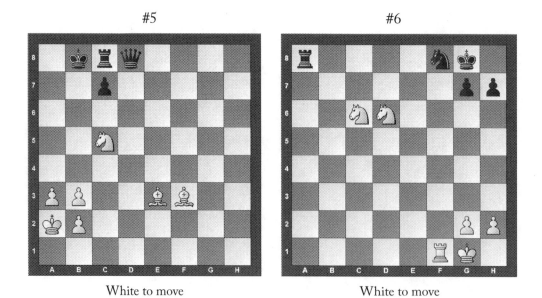

White to move   White to move

#7

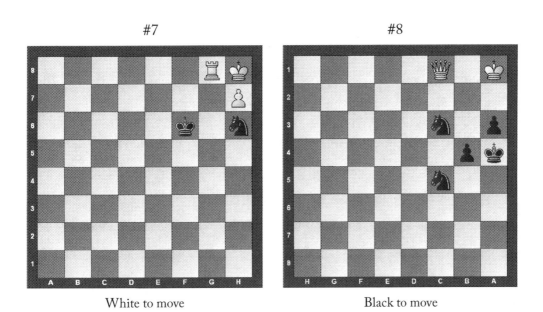

White to move

#8

Black to move

#9

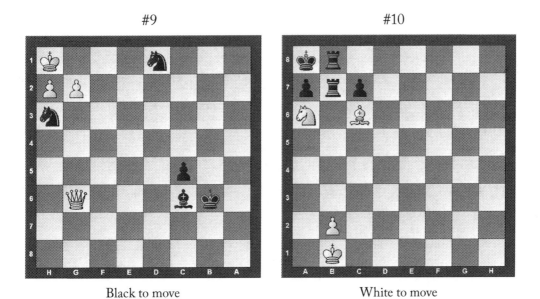

Black to move

#10

White to move

18. Pawn Mate

A *pawn mate* is a checkmate that is delivered by a pawn.

#1   #2

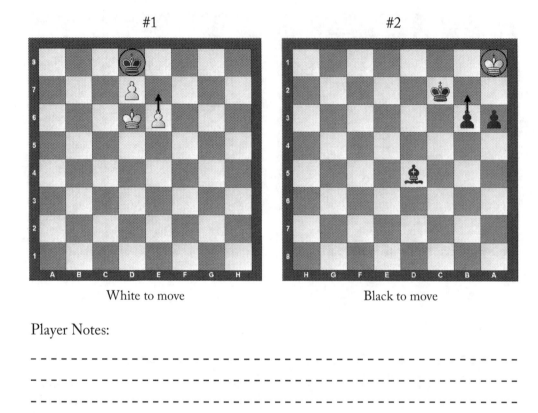

White to move   Black to move

Player Notes:

- -
- -
- -

#3

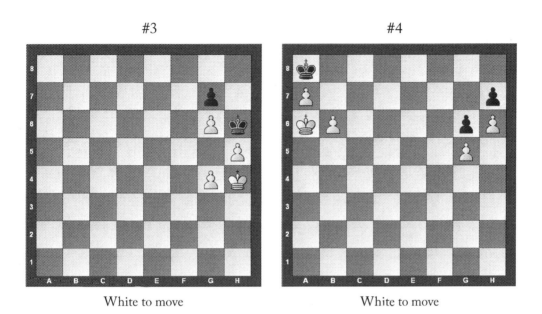

White to move

#4

White to move

#5

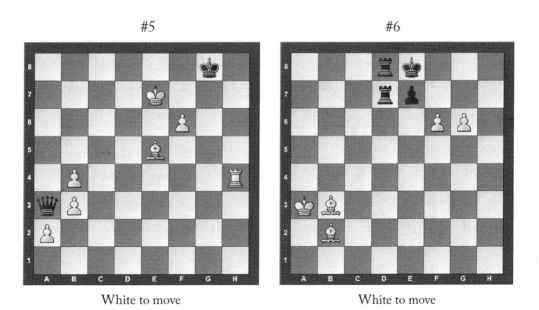

White to move

#6

White to move

#7

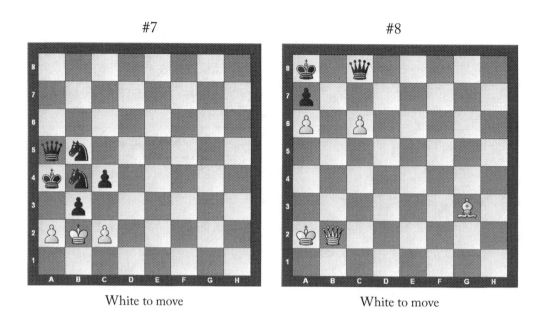

White to move

#8

White to move

#9

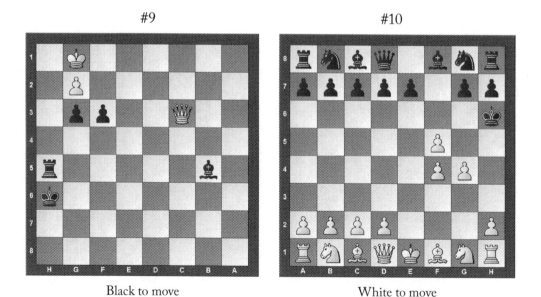

Black to move

#10

White to move

19. Boden's Mate

Boden's mate is a checkmating pattern in chess when both bishops work together to checkmate the king. One blocks off one diagonal while the other checks the king. The other squares near the king are blocked off by its own pieces

#1   #2

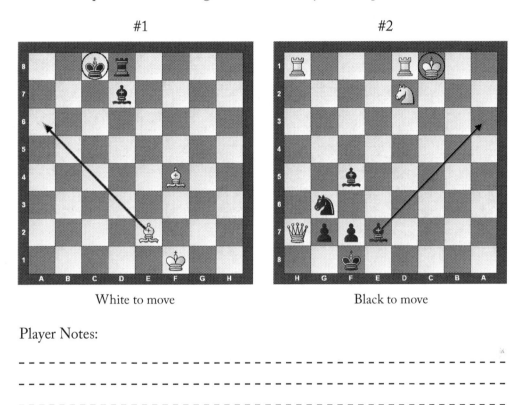

White to move   Black to move

Player Notes:

- -

- -

- -

#3

#4

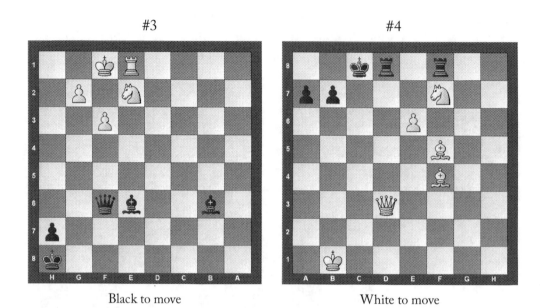

Black to move   White to move

#5

#6

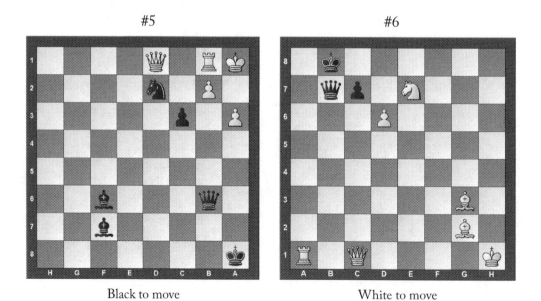

Black to move   White to move

#7

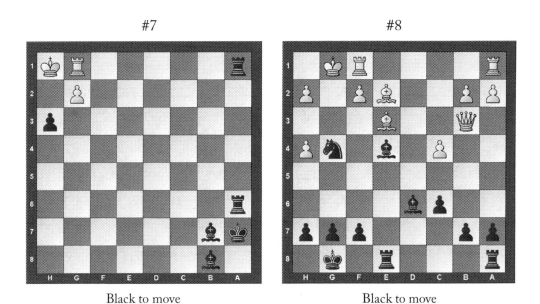

Black to move

#8

Black to move

#9

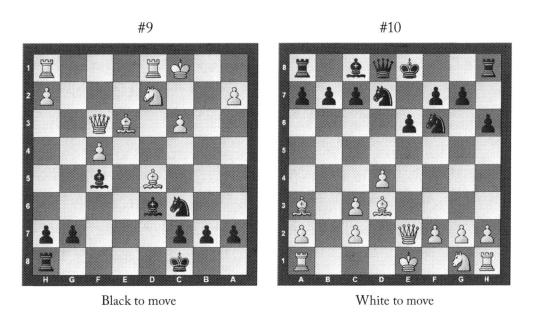

Black to move

#10

White to move

20. Arabian Mate

In an *Arabian mate*, the rook and knight work together to checkmate the king. The rook checks the king while the knight blocks it off.

#1   #2

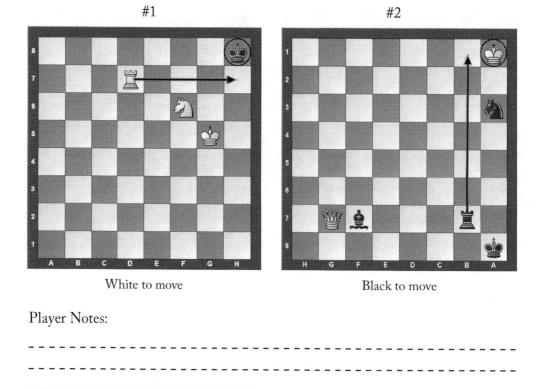

White to move   Black to move

Player Notes:

- -

- -

- -

#3

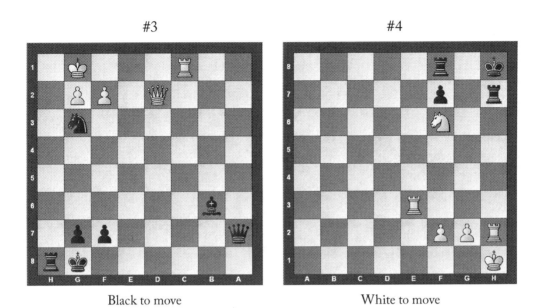

Black to move

#4

White to move

#5

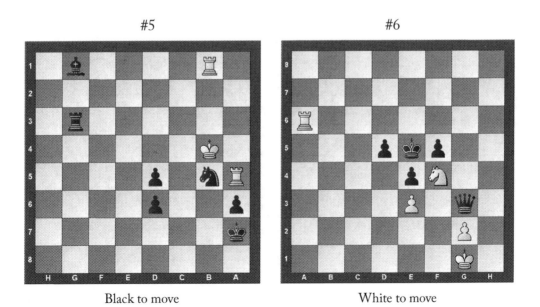

Black to move

#6

White to move

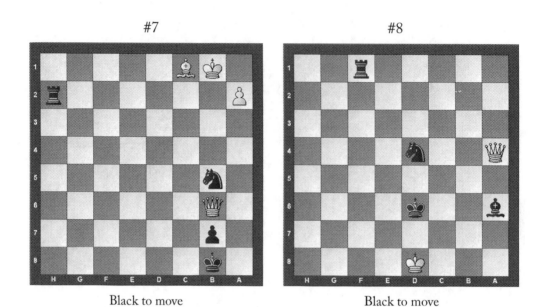

#7

Black to move

#8

Black to move

#9

White to move

#10

Black to move

21. Anderssen's Mate

This mating pattern is formed when the opponent's king is in the first or last rank, and there is a pawn in front of it. Then one of the rooks or the queen goes diagonal from the pawn and delivers checkmate.

#1   #2

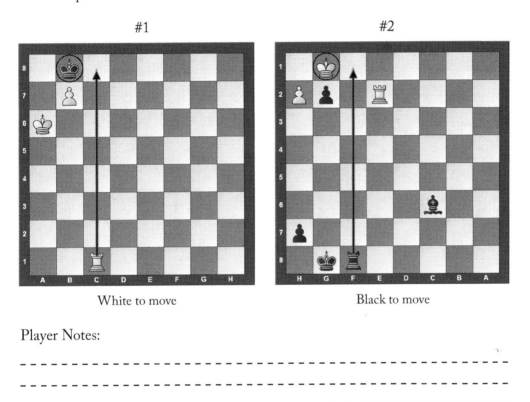

White to move   Black to move

Player Notes:

- -

- -

- -

#3

#4

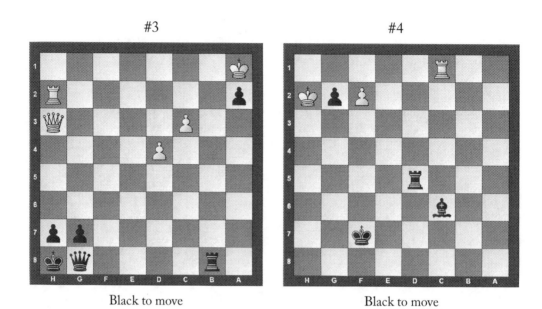

Black to move

Black to move

#5

#6

White to move

Black to move

#7

#8

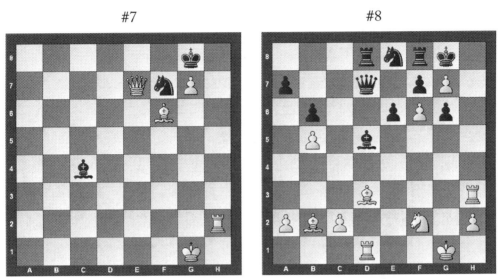

White to move   White to move

#9

#10

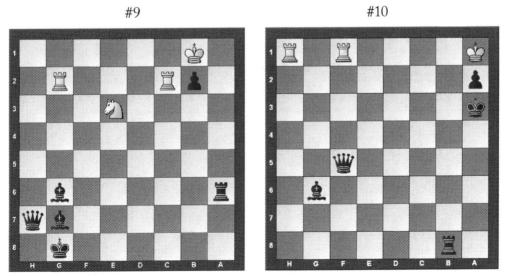

Black to move   Black to move

22. Anastasia's Mate

Anastasia's mate is a variation on the simple rook-knight checkmating pattern and mating net with an open *h* or *a* file.

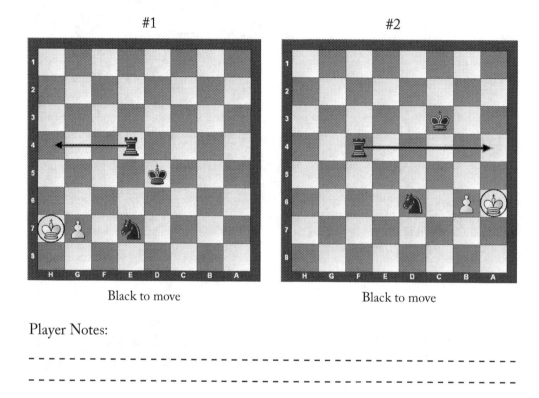

#1   #2

Black to move   Black to move

Player Notes:

- -

- -

- -

#3

#4

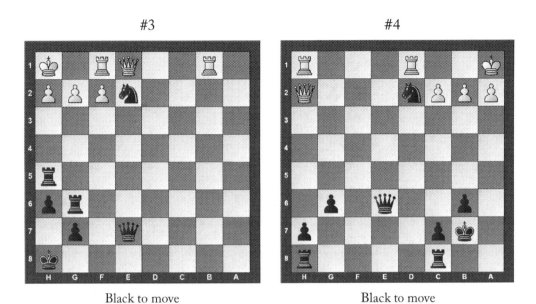

Black to move

Black to move

#5

#6

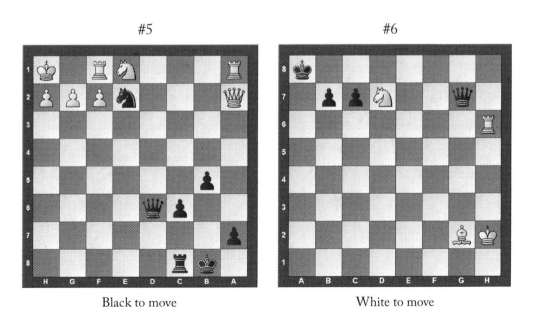

Black to move

White to move

#7

#8

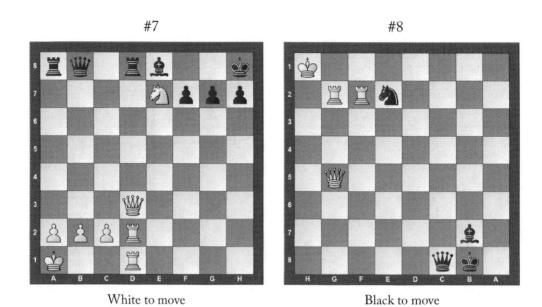

White to move   Black to move

#9

#10

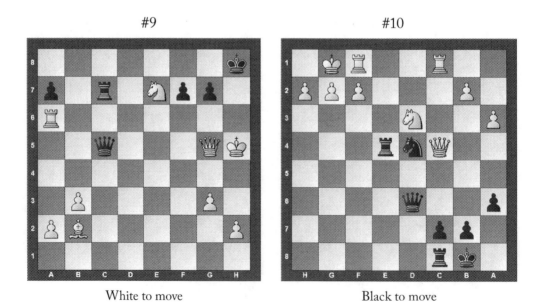

White to move   Black to move

23. Morphy's Mate

This is a checkmate conducted by a bishop and a rook or queen. The rook or queen blocks the king off, and the bishops delivers checkmate.

#1

#2

White to move

Black to move

Player Notes:

- -
- -
- -

#3

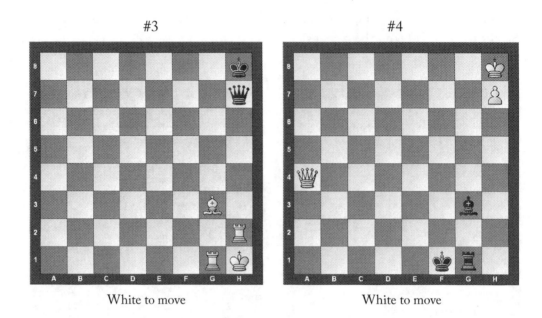

White to move

#4

White to move

#5

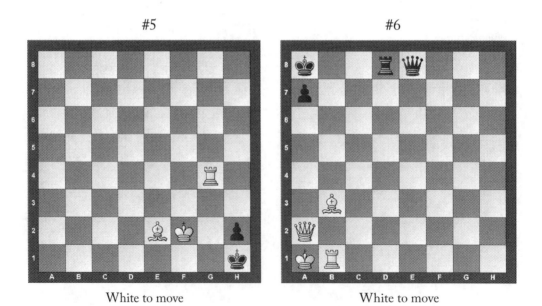

White to move

#6

White to move

#7

#8

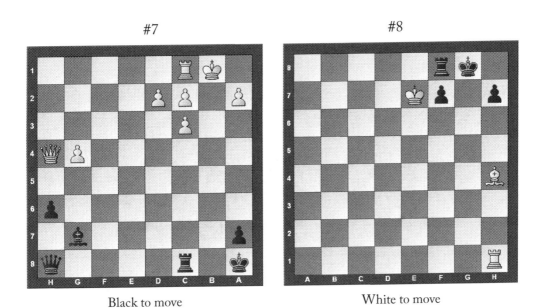

Black to move

White to move

#9

#10

Black to move

White to move

24. Smothered Mate

In chess, a *smothered mate* is a checkmate delivered by a knight in which the mated king is unable to move because he is surrounded by his own pieces.

#1   #2

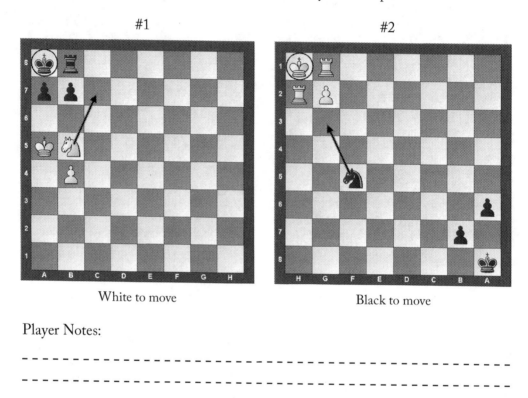

White to move   Black to move

Player Notes:

- -

- -

- -

#3

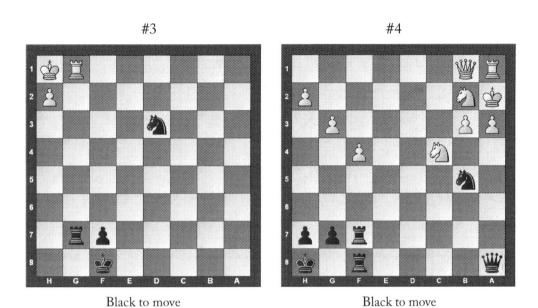

Black to move

#5

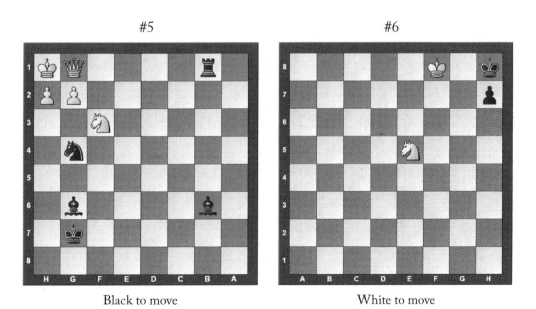

Black to move

#4

Black to move

#6

White to move

#7

#8

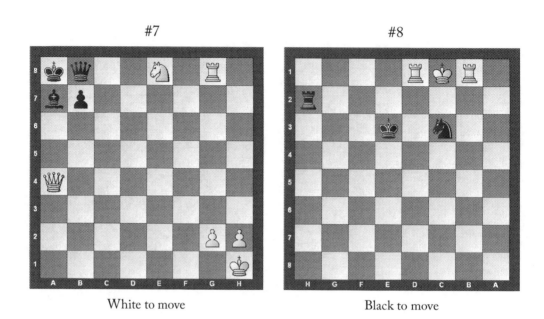

White to move

Black to move

#9

#10

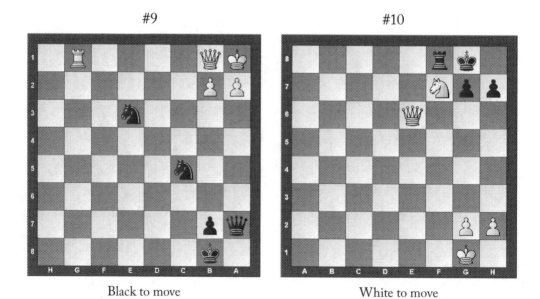

Black to move

White to move

Chess Quiz #3

1. What is checkmate?
2. What is a piece called that cannot move and is under attack?
3. How many pieces are needed to checkmate?
4. Which checkmate uses the first or eighth rank?
5. What piece does the smothered mate use?
6. What happens when you don't say "Adjust" and you touch a piece?
7. What happens when your time runs out?
8. What tactic moves a piece to give another piece more mobility?
9. Can you have more than two queens on the board?
10. How do you tie when you do not offer a draw or agree to one?

CHAPTER 4
ADVANCED CHESS PUZZLES

♖ ♘ ♗ ♔ ♕ ♘ ♙

25. Opposition

Opposition is when the two kings are directly in front of each other, and there is only one square in between. When this occurs, the player whose move it is has a disadvantage.

#1

Black to move

#2

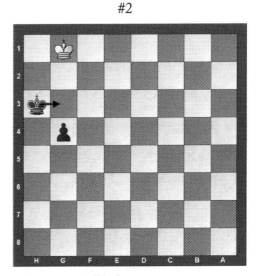

Black to move

Player Notes:

- -
- -
- -

#3

#4

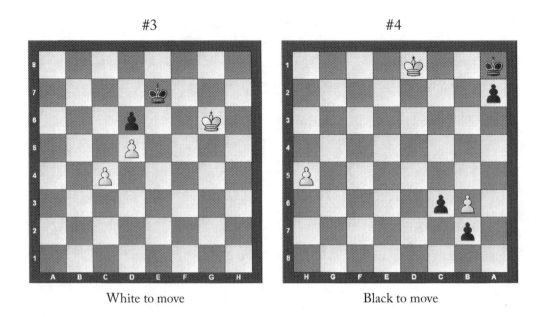

White to move

Black to move

#5

#6

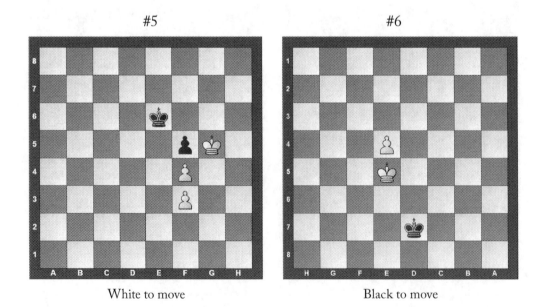

White to move

Black to move

#7

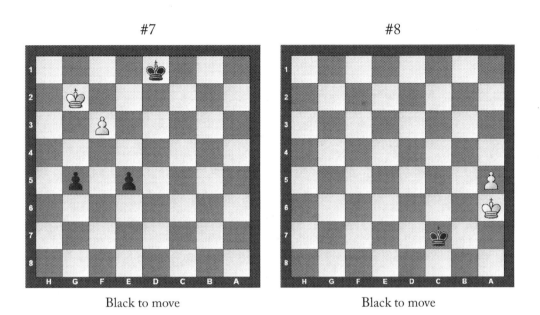

Black to move

#8

Black to move

#9

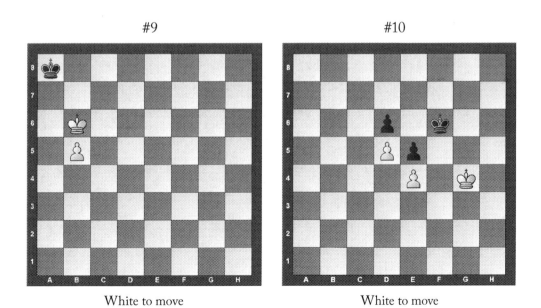

White to move

#10

White to move

26. X-Ray

An *X-ray* involves a piece putting pressure on one piece that it is directly hitting and the piece behind it.

#1   #2

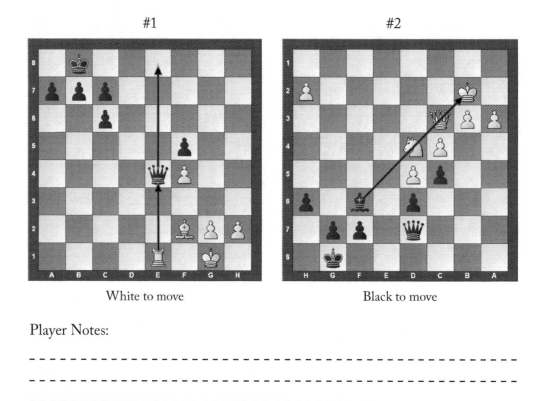

White to move   Black to move

Player Notes:

- -

- -

- -

#3

#4

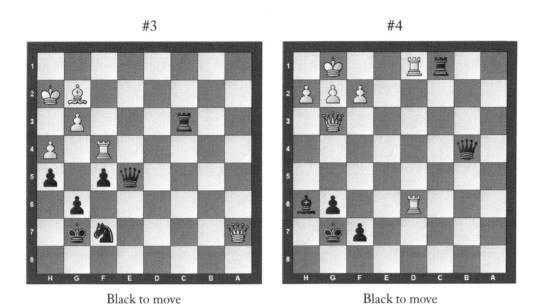

Black to move   Black to move

#5

#6

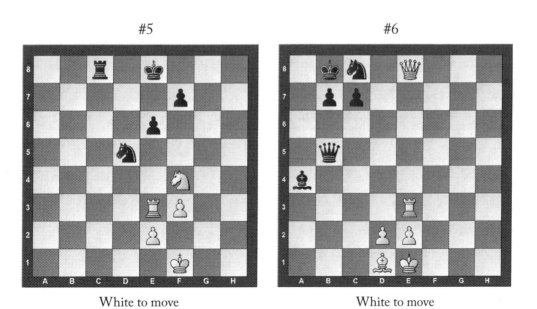

White to move   White to move

#7

#8

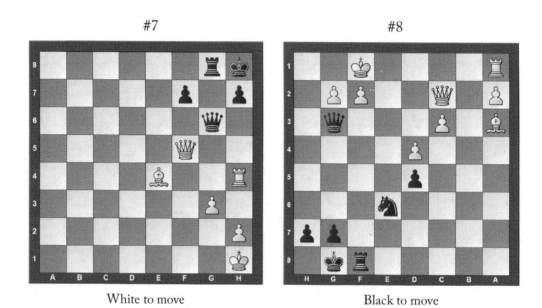

White to move

Black to move

#9

#10

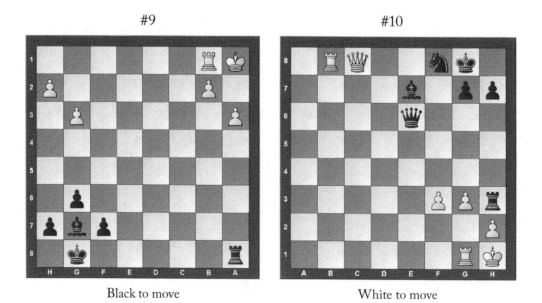

Black to move

White to move

27. Mixed Tactics

These puzzles use a combination of tactics and mates to see if you have learned them from previous pages.

#1   #2

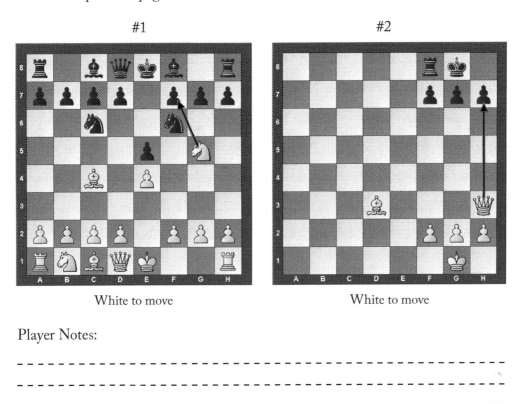

White to move   White to move

Player Notes:

#3

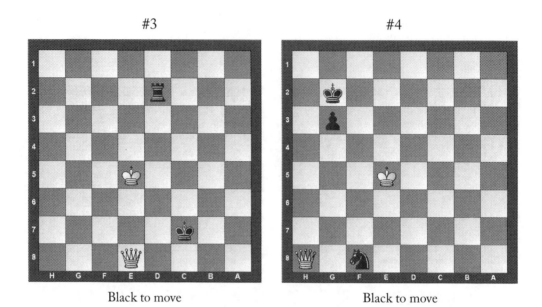

Black to move

#4

Black to move

#5

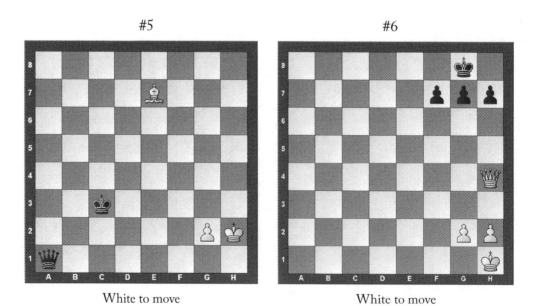

White to move

#6

White to move

#7

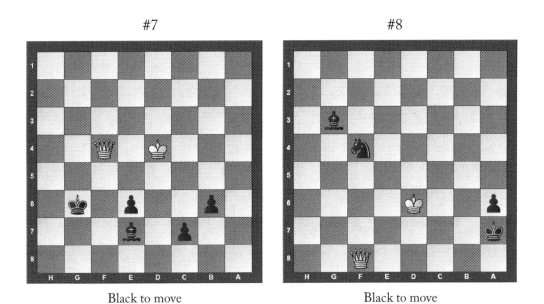

Black to move

#8

Black to move

#9

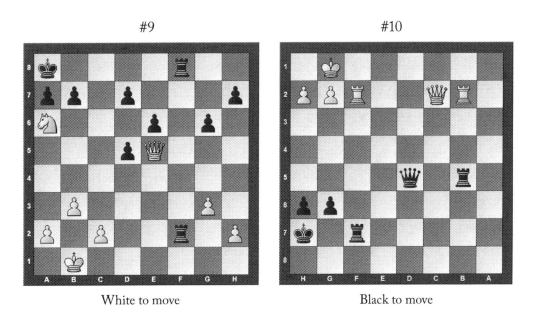

White to move

#10

Black to move

28. Greek Gift

This is a bishop sack that usually happens on h7 or h2. It gives the player a great deal of compensation for the piece.

#1   #2

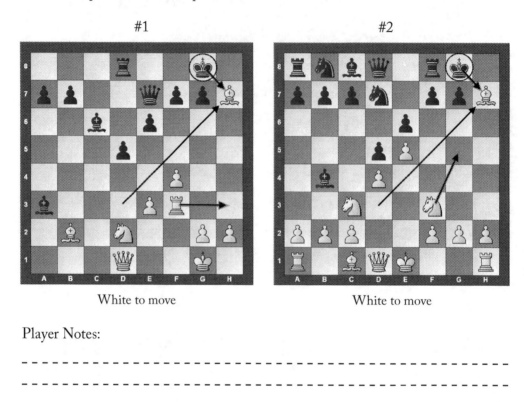

White to move   White to move

Player Notes:

#3

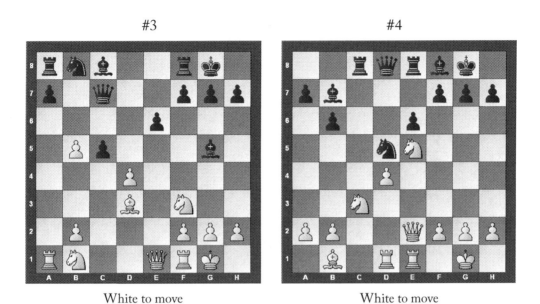

White to move

#4

White to move

#5

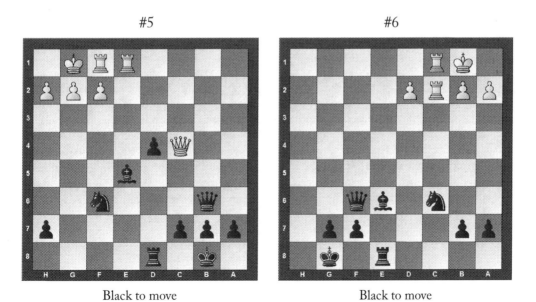

Black to move

#6

Black to move

#7

#8

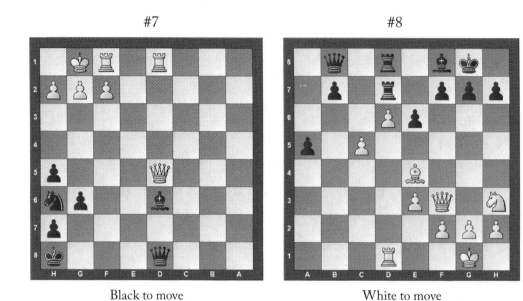

Black to move   White to move

#9

#10

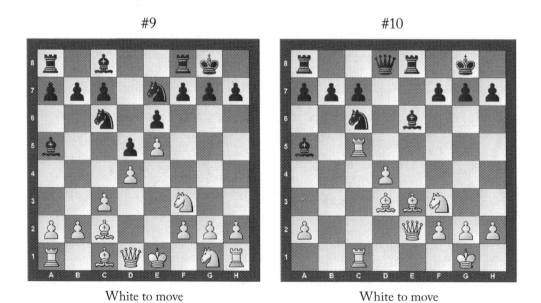

White to move   White to move

29. Stalemate

A *stalemate* is a forced draw. This happens when one player has no legal moves. Only in a losing position would a player want this to happen.

#1   #2

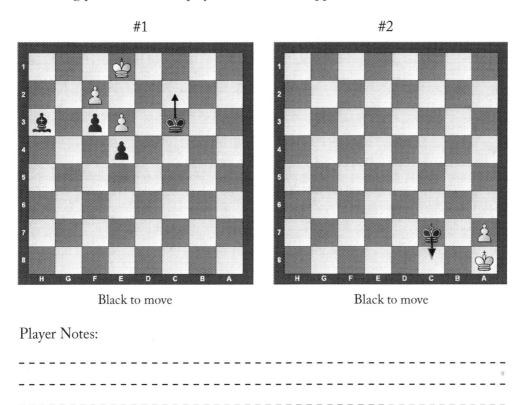

Black to move   Black to move

Player Notes:

- -

- -

- -

#3

#4

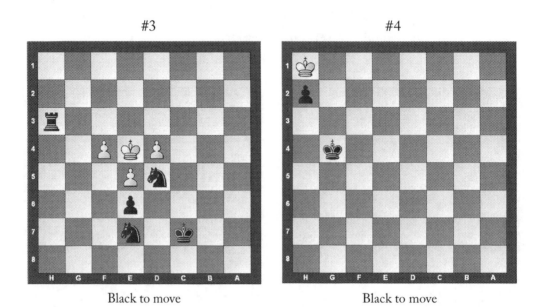

Black to move   Black to move

#5

#6

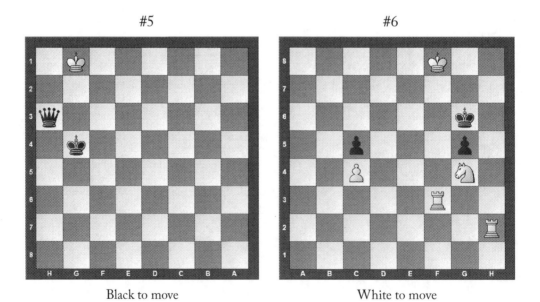

Black to move   White to move

#7

#8

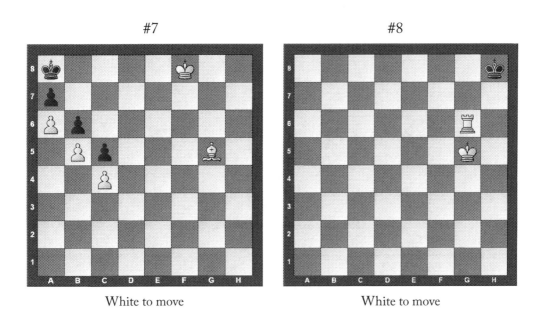

White to move

White to move

#9

#10

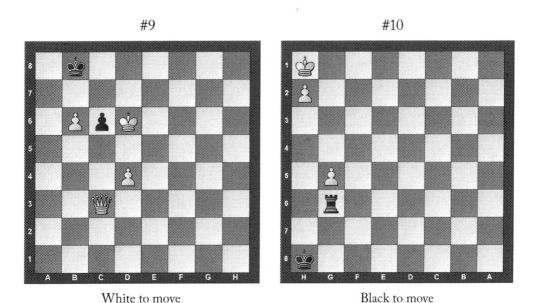

White to move

Black to move

30. Zugzwang

This is a situation that a player would want to put an opponent in. The player who has zugzwang has no good moves or any moves to improve the position. The opponent needs to find a way to put the other player in zugzwang. In the puzzles below, say which player is in zugzwang.

#1   #2

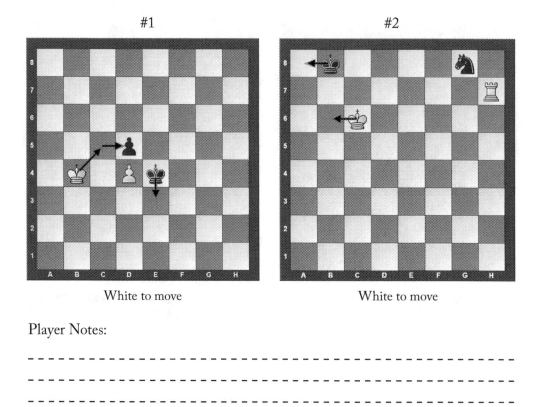

White to move   White to move

Player Notes:

- -
- -
- -

#3

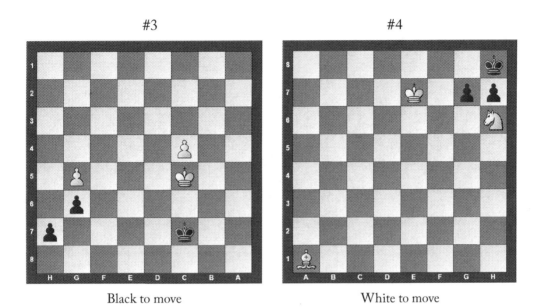

Black to move   White to move

#5

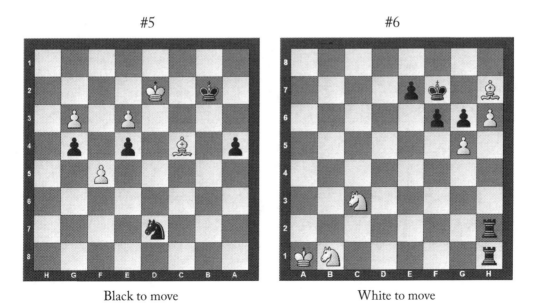

Black to move   White to move

#7

#8

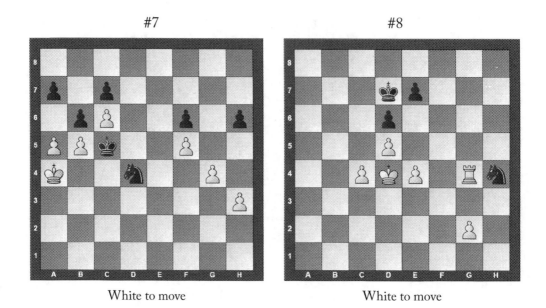

White to move   White to move

#9

#10

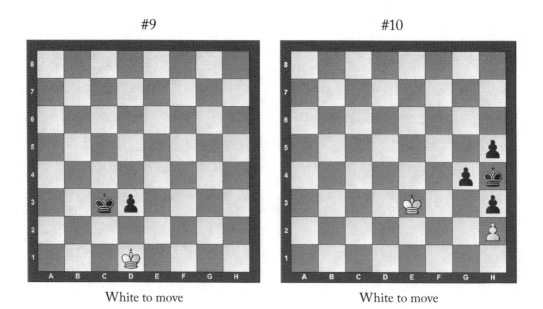

White to move   White to move

Chess Quiz #4

1. What pieces can a pawn not promote to?
2. What piece can you not deliver a checkmate with?
3. What is zugzwang?
4. Where do back rank tactics happen?
5. Who wins when you make a stalemate?
6. What piece is used in opposition?
7. Does the tactic Greek gift involve a sacrifice?
8. When is it good to sacrifice?
9. Order of piece values least to greatest?
10. What does the notation # mean?

CHAPTER 5
TRAPS

#1 – Fishing Pole

This trap could occur in several different openings. It is very common, and all options are equally deadly. It is a knight sack that, if taken, leads to checkmate. The knight sack allows the queen to get in the action and at the same time block off the king.

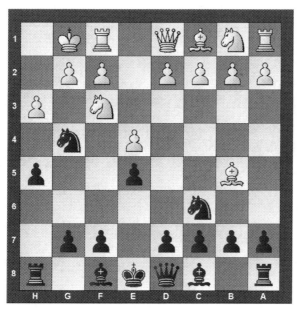

1. e4 e5 2. Nf3 Nc6 3. Bb5 Nf6 4. O-O Ng4 5. h3 h5

#2 – Lasker Trap

This trap could be devastating if an opponent falls into it. If the opponent plays the most obvious move to take the bishop, then the opposing player takes the pawn with check. It is all downhill from there. Then he is forced to move his king up, or he will hang his queen. When that happens, the player proceeds to take the opponent's knight with check because it will be promoted to a knight.

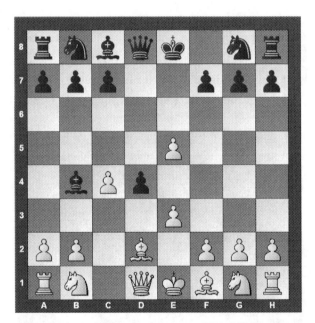

1. d4 d5 2. c4 e5 3. dxe5 d4 4. e3 Bb4 5. Bd2 dxe3
6. Bxb4 6 ... exf2 7. Ke2 fxg1=N 8. Ke1 Qh4+ 9. Kd2 Nc6

#3 – Cambridge Springs Trap

This is very popular because it is out of the queen's gambit, which is a well-played opening. It is also very easily mistaken as an error because the queen is hanging.

1. d4 d5 2. c4 e6 3. Nc3 Nf6 4. Bg5 Nbd7 5. Nf3 c6 6. e3 Qa5

#4 – Blackburn Shillings Trap

This trap comes out of the Italian game opening. It is very easy for white to fall into because all of black's moves seem random at the moment. This breaks many opening principles, but if it is fallen into, it will be devastating for white.

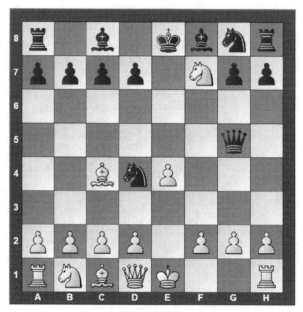

1. e4 e5 2. Nf3 Nc6 3. Bc4 Nd4 4. Nxe5 Q g5 5. Nxf7 Qxg2 6. Rf1 Qxe4 7. Bf2 Nf2#

#5 – Legal Trap

This trap comes from a very typical opening, but if fallen into, it leads to mate. After the trap is set, the most obvious move on the entire board is to take the hanging queen. If black proceeds to do so, white checkmates.

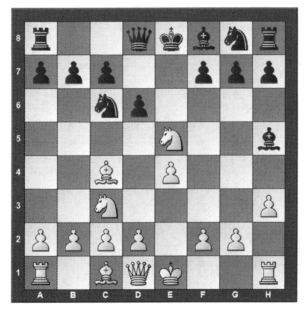

1. e4 e5 2. Nf3 Nc6 3. Bc4 d6 4. Nc3 Bg4?! 5. Nxe5 Bxd1 6. Bxf7+ Ke7 7. Nd5#

#6 – Noah's Ark Trap

This trap comes from the Ruy Lopez, which is probably the most common opening. This trap catches white's light-square bishop.

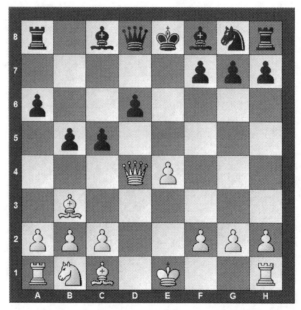

1. e4 e5 2. Nf3 Nc6 3. Bb5 a6 4. Ba4 d6 5. d4 b5 6. Bb3 Nxd4
7. Nxd4 exd4 8. Qxd4 c5 9. Qd5 Be6 10. Qc6+ Bd7 11. Qd5 c4

#7 – Siberian Trap

This trap comes out of the Smith-Morra gambit. In this trap, the player is either forced to lose a queen or forced into checkmate.

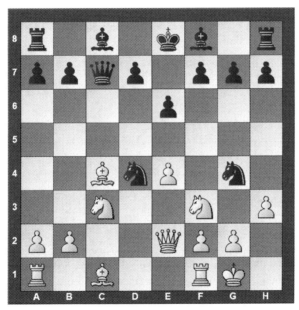

1. e4 c5 2. d4 cxd4 3. c3 dxc3 4. Nxc3 Nc6
5. Nf3 e6 6. Bc4 Qc7 7. 0-0 Nf6 8. Qe2 Ng4 9. h3 Nd4

#8 – Rubinstein Trap

This trap comes out of the queen's gambit. Unlike most of the other traps, if they do not fall into this trap, opposing players still win a pawn at the very least.

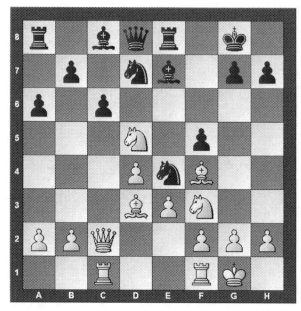

1. d4 d5 2. Nf3 Nf6 3. c4 e6 4. Bg5 Ndb7 5. e3 Be7 6. Nc3 0-0 7. Rc1 Re8
8. Qc2 a6 9. cxd5 exd5 10. Bd3 c6 11. 0-0 ne4 12. Bf4 f5 13. Nxd5 cxd5 14. Bc7

#9 – Englund Gambit Trap

This opening is called the Englund gambit. It is a very tricky trap, because all of the moves leading up to the trap seem normal. The end result is checkmate.

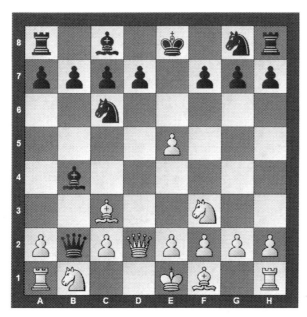

1. d5 e5 2. dxe5 Nc6 3. Nf3 Qe7 4. Bf4 Qb4
5. Bd2 Qxb2 6. Bc3 Bb4 7. Qd2 Bxc3 8. Qxc3 Qc1#

#10 – Fajarowicz Trap

This trap comes out of the Budapest opening. In this trap, a player sacrifices two minor pieces for a queen.

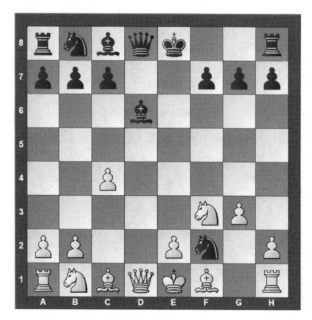

1. d4 Nf6 2. c4 e5 3. dxe4 Ne4 4. Nf3 d6 5. exd6 Bxd6 6. g3 Nxf2 7. Kxf2 Bxg3

CHAPTER 6
TIPS

Tip #1

Un-castled king is like an open door in a bad neighborhood.—Karthik Murugan

Tip #2

Play the opening like a book, the middle game like a magician, and the endgame like a machine.—Rudolph Spielmann

Tip #3

One doesn't have to play well, it's enough to play better than your opponent.—Siegbert Tarrasch

Tip #4

One bad move nullifies forty good ones.—Bernhard Horwitz

Tip #5

If your opponent offers you a draw, try to work out why he thinks he is worse off.—Nigel Short

Tip #6

When you see a good move, look for a better one.—Emanuel Lasker

Tip #7

Even a poor plan is better than no plan at all.—Mikhail Chigorin

Tip #8

I prefer to lose a really good game than to win a bad one.—David Levy

Tip #9

I don't believe in psychology. I believe in good moves.—Bobby Fischer

Tip #10

Modern chess is too much concerned with things like pawn structure. Forget it, checkmate ends the game.—Nigel Short

Tip #11

You may learn much more from a game you lose than from a game you win. You will have to lose hundreds of games before becoming a good player.—Jose Raul Capablanca

Tip #12

Nobody ever won a chess game by resigning.—Savielly Tartakower

CHAPTER 7
STRATEGY

General Strategy

1. Control the center.
2. Develop your pieces before you start attacking.
3. Secure the king.
4. Avoid premature attack.
5. Eliminate the opponent's key pieces.
6. When holding material advantage, simplify the game.
7. Avoid isolated or doubled pawns.
8. Avoid having any unprotected pieces.
9. Look for a good move, then find a better one.
10. Don't make a move until examining every single move or capture.
11. Try to anticipate what an opponent's game plan is before making a move.
12. Don't leave your pieces unprotected. Trade only if it is advantageous.

Opening Strategy

1. Control the center (d4, d5, e4, e5).
2. Develop minor pieces (bishop, knight).
3. Secure the kings.
4. Try not to move the same piece twice.
5. Don't fall for four-move checkmate.
6. Don't aggressively advance pawns in front of a castled king
7. Don't bring the queen out early without a good reason. This will be a waste of time moving it to safety while the opponent continues developing pieces and gaining space.

8. Avoid premature attacks.
9. Don't complicate things; pick one popular opening that's easy to remember and play it until it is second nature. Don't neglect development of your pieces.

Midgame Strategy

1. Don't ignore potential attacks on f2 (white) or f7 (black) early in the game.
2. Don't fall for the knight fork.
3. Don't isolate pawns.
4. Keep the king secured in midgame. Bring it to the center in endgame.
5. Don't get into a cramped position.
6. Consider taking an opponent's pieces that are not safe or are unprotected. Don't ignore the king's safety.
7. Don't neglect development of pieces.
8. Don't leave pieces unprotected.
9. Don't waste moves by making moves that have no point or giving check without a good reason.
10. Trade only if it is advantageous.
11. Consider what the opponent is trying to do after each move.
12. Make sure all your pieces are doing something all the time.

Endgame Strategy

1. Pawns become more important.
2. Centralize the king as quickly as possible in the endgame.
3. The king must be active in the endgame.
4. Keep rooks active in the endgame.
5. Try to place a rook behind a passed pawn.
6. Centralize the queen in the endgame.
7. Don't overlook mating threats or possible attacks against the king.
8. Make sure all pieces are doing something all the time.

CHESS QUIZ ANSWERS

Quiz 1

1. Sixty-four
2. Thirty-two
3. White
4. L
5. Diagonal
6. It can promote
7. Checkmate, resignation, flag, forfeit
8. White color
9. Pawn and knight
10. Checkmate

Quiz 2

1. One piece attacking two pieces at the same time
2. Knight
3. Draw
4. Queen, rook, bishop, knight
5. Deflection
6. Discovered attack
7. Fork
8. Lower value is in front with pin, in back with skewer
9. Bishop, rook, queen
10. Bishop, queen

Quiz 3

1. King cannot move and is under check which cannot be stopped
2. Trapped piece
3. Two or more
4. Back rank

5. Knight
6. The piece has to be moved
7. Forfeit
8. Clearance
9. Yes
10. Stalemate, three move repetitions

Quiz 4

1. King, pawn
2. King
3. When all your moves are bad
4. First and eighth rank
5. No one; it's a draw.
6. King
7. Yes
8. When you get something back in return eventually
9. Pawn, knight, bishop rook, queen, king
10. Checkmate

REFERENCES

Chess Websites

Chess.com
Lichess.Org
Chesstempo.com
TheChessWebsite.org
Chessclub.com
Chess24.com

Chess Books

How to Beat Your Dad at Chess by Murray Chandler
Chess for Children by Murray Chandler and Helen Milligan
Chess Puzzles for Kids by Murray Chandler
Bobby Fischer Teaches Chess by Stuart Margulies, Bobby Fischer, and Don Mosenfelder
Winning Chess Puzzles for Kids by Jeff Coakley
Winning Chess Exercises for Kids by Jeff Coakley
Winning Chess Strategy for Kids by Jeff Coakley

Basic Tournament Rules

- Touch move: If a player touches a piece, it has to be moved.
- Touch take: If a player touches the opponent's piece, it must be taken.
- Adjust: A player has to say "Adjust" before centering a piece or else the above two rules apply.
- Clock: If time runs out, the player will lose the game.
- No notation is necessary when the game is under five minutes.
- An illegal move should be called out and given two minutes or half time off, whichever is less.
- No talking during a game unless a player resigns, offers a draw, or says "Check."
- Shake hands with an opponent before and after the game.

- If you or your opponent makes an illegal move without calling it, after you and your opponent play a move after that, the move goes away.
- If the opponent offers a draw and a move is played after that, the draw offer is gone.

SOLUTIONS

* prefix indicates other possible solutions.

1. Fork

1. Nxf7
2. Bxd5+
3. Ne5+
4. d4
5. Rd4
6. Rxc5, Rxc5, Nd3+
7. Qc7+
8. Nc6+
9. Nc2+
10. Rc3+, Kxc3, d4+

2. Pin

1. Bg5
2. Bc6
3. Bb5
4. Bxg8
5. Re8
6. Bb4
7. Bf8
8. Qa1
9. Bg7
10. Rc1+, Kg2, Bc6

3. Skewer

1. Bg7+
2. Bc7
3. Rb3+
4. Rh1+
5. Qe8+, Kh7, Qa8
6. Nf3+, Bxf3, Rg8+
7. Bg4
8. Rh7+, Nxh7, Rxh7+
9. Bxd4+, Qxd4, Qh8+
10. Bb4

4. Discovered Attack

1. Nxf3+
2. Bxc3+
3. Kf5+
4. Ng6+
5. *Rd1+
6. Nf6+
7. Nf6+
8. Nd3+
9. *c8=Q+
10. Rxe3+

5. Back Rank

1. Rd8#
2. Qd1#
3. Qd8#
4. Re1+, Qxe1, Rxe1#
5. Q g8+, Qc8, Qxc8#
6. Bxe4+, dxe4, Rd1#
7. Q g1+, Bd1, Qxd1#
8. Qxg8+, Nxg8, Rf8#
9. Rxe3, dxe3, Rd1#
10. Be6+, Kb8, Rxd8#

6. Deflection

1. Bxc6+
2. Rxb3
3. Qxe6
4. *Bc4+
5. Qc4+
6. *Nxd5
7. Qxc3
8. *Rxc1+
9. Bxa2+
10. Qg8+

7. Clearance

1. Be4+
2. Bd2+
3. Bxb2+
4. Qxh7
5. Qxc6+
6. Rf8+, Qxf8, Qxh7#
7. Qh3
8. Qxf7+
9. Qxf6
10. Qh2+

8. Pawn Promotion

1. Bc8, Rxc8, Bxc8=Q
2. Rg1, Rxg1, hxg1=Q
3. f7=forced promotion
4. *c2=forced promotion
5. Bg7, Nxg7, f8=Q
6. h7=forced promotion
7. e8=N+, Kc8, Ba6#
8. c7= forced promotion
9. *c7, Rc6, Rb8+, Rxb8, cxb8+=Q
10. *b1=N#

9. Basic Pawn Endings

1. e5, Kd8, Kf7=forced promotion
2. h4, a5, h3, a6, h2, a7, h1=Q, Kc5
3. Kd6, Ke8, Kxe6, Kf8, Kd7=forced promotion
4. e5, Kf7, Kd7
5. Kf2, Kg7, Ke3, Kf7, Kd4, Ke7, Ke5, Kd7, Kd5, Kc7, Ke6, Kc6, d4=forced promotion
6. *Kc5, g4, Kd6, g5, Ke7, g6, Kf6
7. Ke3, a4, Kd4, a5, Kc5, a6, Kb6
8. Kb7, Kd7, a4=forced promotion
9. Kc7, Ka8, Kc8
10. Kf5, Ke8, Ke6, Kd8, d7, Kc7, Ke7

10. Trapped Piece

1. b6
2. c5
3. Bb7
4. Bc3
5. Bd5+
6. Kd6, Be8, Ke7
7. Bg3
8. f3
9. f4
10. c4

11. Basic Mates

1. Rg2+, Kd1, Rh1#
2. Kd3, Kc1, Qc2#
3. Rf7+, Ka8, Kb6, Kb8, Rf8#
4. Qc2+, Kd6, Rd1+, Ke6, Qe2+, Kf6, Rf1+, Kg6, Q g2, Kh6, Rh1#
5. Qa6, Ke7, Qb7+, Ke8, Qa8#
6. Rd8#
7. Q g7#
8. Qh7#
9. Qxg2#
10. Nf2#

12. Mate in One

1. Bxf2#
2. Qxg2#
3. Ng3#
4. Qa1#
5. Bd5#
6. Bxe4#
7. Qf6#
8. Bc6#
9. Re3#
10. Ng2#

13. Mate in Two

1. Rb8+, Rxb8, Rxb8#
2. Rxh7+, Rxh7, Rxh7#
3. Rxc8+, Nxc8, Qd8#
4. Qxh2+, Rxh2, Bxh2#
5. Qxa3+, Qxa3, Bxa3#
6. *Rc1+, Qxc1, Qxc1#
7. Qa4+, Rc6, Qxc6#
8. Be4+, Bd5, Bxd5#
9. Be4+, Qd5, Rc8#
10. Qxh7+, Kf7, Bg6#

14. Queen Mate

1. Qc2#
2. Qxg7#
3. Qc1#
4. Qxf7#
5. Qh4#
6. Qe6#
7. Qxh2+, Kf1, Qh1#
8. Qf1#
9. Qxa2#
10. Rxh2+, Kxh2, Qh4#

15. Rook Mate

1. Re1+, Rd1, Rxd1#
2. Ra8#
3. Re4#
4. Rh8#
5. Rh4#
6. Rh7#
7. Rd1#
8. Re4#
9. Rxg7, Kh8, Rg6, Rf6, Bxf6#
10. Rxb1+, Kxb1, Ra1#

16. Bishop Mate

1. Bc6#
2. Bd4+, Qc3, Bxc3#
3. Ba6#
4. Bxg5#
5. Bh7#
6. Qxc3+, bxc3, Ba3#
7. Bc6#
8. Bc3#
9. Bg7#
10. Bb2#

17. Knight Mate

1. Nf7#
2. Nd7#
3. *Nf2#
4. *Ndc2+, Qxc2, Nxc2#
5. Na6#
6. Ne7+, Kh8, Nf7#
7. Nf7#
8. Nb3#
9. Ndf2#
10. Nxc7#

18. Pawn Mate

1. e7#
2. b2#
3. g5#
4. b7#
5. f7#
6. f7+, Kf8, g7#
7. *cxb3+, cxb3, axb3#
8. Qb7+, Qxb7, cxb7#
9. f2#
10. g5#

19. Boden's Mate

1. Ba6#
2. Ba3#
3. Qxf3+, gxf3, Bh3#
4. e7+, Rd7, Bxd7#
5. *cxb2+, Rxb2, Bxb2#
6. dxe7+, Qxc7, Bxc7#
7. *Bxg2#
8. Bxh2#
9. Ba3#
10. Qxe6, fxe6, Bg6#

20. Arabian Mate

1. Rh7#
2. Rb1#
3. Rh1#
4. Rxh7#
5. Bc5+, Ka4, Ra3#
6. Re6#
7. Nc3, Ka1, Rxa2#
8. *Ne6+, Ke8, Rf8#
9. Qxf8, Kxf8, Re8, Kg7, Rg8#
10. Qh2, Kxh2, Ng3, Kg1, Rh1#

21. Anderssen's Mate

1. Rc8#
2. Rf1#
3. Rb1#
4. Rh5+, Kg1, Rh1#
5. Qb8+, Qxb8, Rxb8#
6. Rxf1+, Bxf1, Qg1#
7. Qf8#
8. Rh8#
9. Ra1#
10. Qb1+, Rxb1, Rxb1, Rxb1, axb1 = Q#

22. Anastasia's Mate

1. Rh4#
2. Ra4#
3. Rxh2+, Kxh2, Qh4#
4. Qxa2+, Kxa2, Ra8#
5. Qxh2+, Kxh2, Rh8#
6. Ra6#
7. Qxh7+, Kxh7, Rh1#
8. Qh3#
9. Rh6#
10. Ne2+, Kh1, Qxh2, Kxh2, Rh8#

23. Morphy's Mate

1. Bc6#
2. Bf3#
3. Be5#
4. Be5#
5. Bf3#
6. Bd5+,Rxd5,Qxd5+,Qc6, Qxc6#
7. Rb8+, Ka1, Bxc3+, dxc3, Qxc3#
8. Rg1+, Kh8,Bf6#
9. Qxg2+, Kxg2, Rg8+, Kh1, Bf3#
10. Qxf6,gxf6, Rg3+,Kh8, Bxf6#

24. Smothered Mate

1. Nc7#
2. Ng3#
3. Nf2#
4. Nc3#
5. Nf2#
6. Nf7#
7. Nc7#
8. Na2#
9. Nb3#
10. Nh6+, Kh8, Q g8+, Rxg8, Nf7#

25. Opposition

1. Kd3
2. Kg3
3. Kg7
4. Kb1
5. Kg6, Ke7, Kxf5
6. Ke7
7. Ke2
8. Kc6
9. Ka6
10. Kh5, Kg7, Kg5

26. X-Ray

1. Rxe4
2. Bxd4
3. g5, hxg5, h4
4. Qe1+, Rxe1, Rxe1#
5. Nxd5
6. Bxa4
7. Qf6+, Qxf6, Rxh7#
8. Nxd4, cxd4, Qxa3
9. Rxa3#
10. Qxe6+

27. Mixed Tactics

1. Nxf7
2. Qxh7#
3. Re2+
4. Ng6+
5. Bf6+
6. Qd8#
7. e5+, Qxe5, Bf6
8. Ng6+
9. Qb8+, Rxb8, Nc7#
10. Rxb2,Qxb2, Qd1+,Rf1,Qxf1#

28, Greek Gift

1. Kxh7, Rh3+
2. Kxh7, Ng5+
3. Bxh7+, Kxh7, Qe4+
4. Bxh7+, Kxh7, Qh5+
5. Bxh2+, Kxh2, Ng4+
6. Bxa2+, Kxh2, Nb4+
7. *Bxh2+, Kxh2, Qh4+
8. *Bxh7+, Kxh7, Qh5+
9. Bxh7+, Kxh7, Ng5+
10. Bxh7+, Kxh7, Ng5+

29. Stalemate

1. Kc2
2. Kc8
3. Nf5
4. Kg3
5. Kg3
6. Rf7
7. Bf4
8. Kh6
9. Qxc6
10. Rxg5

30. Zugzwang

1. Black
2. Black
3. Black
4. White
5. White
6. White
7. White
8. Black
9. White
10. Black

Printed in the United States
By Bookmasters